Praise for **Re-Storying Education**

"Woven in these pages is a masterful contribution to the field of education and to those who work in educating hearts, minds, and spirits. I found myself lit up, excited, eager to turn each page, and also inspired to slow down, reflect, and let all the beauty in the pages find their rightful place in my own learning. Carolyn Roberts invites us to go on a journey with her, to be in relationship with her as we learn, unlearn, relearn, and ignite our excitement in the joy of education. *Re-Storying Education* is full of knowledge, wisdom, truths, and stories and will influence education for generations to come."

MONIQUE GRAY SMITH,
award-winning and bestselling author of *I Hope*

"An excellent resource for navigating often-fraught waters, turning potential struggle into a hopeful journey of discovery and reconciliation."

EDEN ROBINSON,
bestselling author of the Trickster trilogy

"Carolyn Roberts has created a thought-provoking, easy-to-follow, and foundational guide that draws connections between history, classroom techniques, and, most essentially, her own experiences as a student. *Re-Storying Education* demonstrates the importance of belonging and community in education. Carolyn invites you to reflect on how your classroom experiences have shaped you and to reflect on your role in maintaining the status quo or pushing the bounds of what we think a classroom can be.

Through her personal stories, she shows the profound impact our time as a student can have on us in how we understand ourselves and others. Carolyn aptly explains the importance of making students feel they belong, instead of telling them they're 'right' or 'wrong,' and her respect for students shines through. This book brings together the deepness of personal stories, the expertise of an educator, and hope for the future."

STEPHANIE KWETÁSEL'WET WOOD,
award-winning journalist and reporter at *The Narwhal*

"*Re-Storying Education* is a practical guide for how to support educators in decolonizing their practice. Through storytelling, Carolyn Roberts weaves her own personal experiences and learnings into her writing, providing strategies on how to disrupt and (un)learn stereotypical narratives and 'ways of doing' about Indigenous Peoples by creating space to Re-Story the present and the future. Each chapter starts with a creative musical playlist to uniquely connect each of the chapters' learnings and ends with critical reflective questions and a resource list. I highly recommend this important resource for all educators but in particular those teaching in the K–12 system. What a wonderful book!"

SHEILA COTE-MEEK, PhD,
author of *Colonized Classrooms: Racism, Trauma and Resistance in Post-Secondary Education*

CAROLYN ROBERTS

Re-Storying Education

Decolonizing Your Practice Using a Critical Lens

PAGE TWO

Cataloguing in publication information
is available from Library and Archives Canada.
ISBN 978-1-77458-496-5 (paperback)
ISBN 978-1-77458-497-2 (ebook)

Page Two
pagetwo.com

Edited by Kendra Ward
Copyedited by Rachel Taylor
Proofread by Alison Strobel
Cover and interior design by Fiona Lee
Cover illustration by Aaron Nelson-Moody / Tawx'sin Yexwulla, Sḵwx̱wú7mesh Nation
Printed and bound in Canada by Friesens
Distributed in Canada by Raincoast Books
Distributed in the US and internationally by Macmillan

24 25 26 27 28 5 4 3 2 1

carolynroberts.net

This book is dedicated to my children, who are my reason for everything I do. I love you all to the moon and back. It is also for all of those who struggle in education systems. I see you and want to give you the education you deserve.

Contents

A Note from the Author

STORIES SURROUND US and shape who we are. We all come from the stories we tell about ourselves and our life experiences. Our stories include the stories we share and the stories we learn from. Our stories are about our upbringings, our families, our ancestors, and the land; our stories tell us about who we are as people. I think of Re-Storying as a way to look back and reflect on what has come before us and as an opportunity to change the story going forward. Re-Storying Education is a process of dismantling old narratives to rebuild and Re-Story new narratives to include historically silenced voices in education, to make space for all stories of this place to be told.

Dwayne Donald[1] and Leanne Betasamosake Simpson[2] define colonization as the severing of relationships. Severing and separating from each other, the land, the waterways, our communities, and the more-than-human. One way to repair the devasting impacts of colonization is through a rebuilding of connection and through the Re-Storying of this place. By connecting education as a wholistic practice, and rebuilding connections with one another, the land, the waterways, our communities, and the more-than-human, we can start to Re-Story: to rebuild a relationship to education and to the stories that we have been told. Within the western colonial education system, the western colonial story has been dominant, and it has excluded so many other stories that have built this place known as Canada today. Re-Storying is including and making space for historically silenced voices in the education system so that we can build a complete story of this place we all live in, the whole shared history.

In Canada, I believe that this book is critical for this moment in time. Educators are being asked to implement Indigenous history, Indigenous education, and Indigenous pedagogy into their practice, with mandatory Indigenous course requirements becoming the norm in provinces. My experiences using Indigenous pedagogies in the classroom for over twenty years—including as an educator in two different teacher education programs (one at Simon Fraser University and the other at the University of the Fraser Valley) for the last five years, and working with school districts with practising teachers—give me a powerful understanding of what is working in classrooms and how to support educators who are tentative to step into the work of Indigenous education.

My hope is that you find this book an easy read that gives you some insights, thought-provoking questions, and nuggets of knowledge, as though I were sitting at the kitchen table with you having a conversation, like an Aunty. I want to be able to support educators in developing a strong critical lens with what and how they teach in the classroom. I hope this will become a must-have book for new and long-time practising educators all over Canada and beyond.

Welcome

What First Nations people are seeking is not a lesser education, and not even an equal education, but rather a better education—an education that respects them for who they are, that is relevant to their view of the world, that offers reciprocity in their relationships with others, and that helps them exercise responsibility over their own lives.

VERNA KIRKNESS AND RAY BARNHARDT[1]

VERNA KIRKNESS and Ray Barnhardt wrote the paper "First Nations and Higher Education: The Four R's—Respect, Relevance, Reciprocity, Responsibility" in 1991. In it, they demand change within the context of higher education for Indigenous students who were being racially harmed and pushed out of education. What they speak about in this paper is also relevant in higher education and K–12 systems still to this day.

Kirkness and Barnhardt highlight band-aid approaches to supporting Indigenous students, such as giving them extra literacy support, tutoring, counselling, and so on. These approaches reinforce colonial ideals and push students further into assimilation. These approaches do not address the problem within the educational system, which is that the system was not made for Indigenous students to succeed. The system does not include Indigenous knowledge systems, Indigenous cultures, or Indigenous history; therefore, it does not reflect who Indigenous people are, as people. I believe that all students within the education system need to see themselves within the curriculum, within the stories, and within the people who teach them. They need a mirror, a reflection of themselves. They also need windows, which means a space to learn about all other cultures, worldviews, and perspectives within the content they are learning. This idea comes from Dr. Rudine Sims Bishop, from her paper called "Mirrors, Windows, and Sliding Glass Doors."[2] This provides students a bigger understanding of the multiple worldviews, cultures, and lives of all people that they live with. Within this book, I hope to show you some ways that you can support students by offering them mirrors and windows within their learning.

As I sit in my office at home, writing, I am feeling and acknowledging all my ancestors that have come before me in order for me to be here in this moment. In my community, I have been taught that when we get up to speak and share, we first need to acknowledge who we are and whose shoulders we stand upon. These shoulders are the ancestors who have come before us and who speak through us as we share. This critical opening acknowledges and upholds my ancestors and honours their voices, because it is their voices you hear when I speak. I stand upon their shoulders to pass on the knowledge I hold to the next generation.

MY NAME given to me by my birth mother, Janet Baker, is Stacey Lee Baker. The name given to me by the parents who adopted and raised me is Carolyn Hooker (now Roberts). On my mother's side, I am a direct descendant of the hereditary Chief Hunter Jack of the N'Quat'qua Nation; he is my great-great-grandfather. He is the father of Agnus Jack. Agnus Jack and Archie French Thevarge are my great-grandparents; they are the parents of Arthur Thevarge Sr. Arthur Thevarge Sr. and Anna Doss are the parents of my mother, Janet Baker.

My father's side is more complicated as I have just recently reconnected with this side of my family. I am a direct descendant of Tee-kwah-laht-zah from the Stó:lō Nation of Tzeachten. My father is Edward Brenton Kelly; my grandparents are Edward George Kelly and Delivina Walker, whose parents were Joseph Lapoint and Margaret Quilty. I am a member of the Kelly family from the Tzeachten Nation. Under the colonial government and their Indian Act, I am a member of the Squamish Nation because my mother married into the Nation. When my birth mother married her husband (now ex-husband), the Indian Act dictated that she would be removed from her community and become a member of her husband's community. Because of this, I, too, am a member of the Squamish Nation through governmental policy. Squamish Nation is my home community that I feel most connected to. I come from a long line of Indigenous people who have lived with and on these lands since time out of mind. It is colonially known today as southern British Columbia (BC).

I am also a child of the Sixties Scoop. This refers to the Canadian governmental practice, in place from the 1960s to the 1980s, of removing Indigenous children from their homes and adopting them into non-Indigenous homes as a way to assimilate them into the western, european culture. I was stolen from my mother and community at birth. Through my matriarchal lines, I am St'at'imc from the Thevarge family of the N'Quat'qua Nation. On my father's side, I am Stó:lō from the Kelly family of the Tzeachten Nation. I returned back home in my early twenties and began my journey to re-member who I am and whose shoulders I stand upon in the work I do as an educator and speaker. I come to this work with a deeply rooted connection to my ancestors, as their blood and blood memory run deeply through my veins.

THE WORK you are reading is a product of all my ancestors and the scholars who have come before me who fought back to tell their stories with their words and through their writing. It is because of their fearlessness and relentlessness to write in the colonizing language and in colonized spaces that I can do this work today. As I step into this history of writing as a witness to those Indigenous educators who are doing the work today, I, too, am creating the space for those who will come after me.

I would like to take a moment to explain my thinking and reasons for capitalizations in this work. I have purposefully not capitalized certain words, such as "european" and "western," in my writing. As an Indigenous academic, I am working through how to decolonize in so many ways, and not capitalizing these terms reflects that thinking and learning. It is a way to acknowledge the struggle for Indigenous recognition within the hierarchies of the western knowledge systems and writing in the english language; just as capitalizing "Indigenous" is a way to show respect for the struggle of recognition for Indigenous people within these systems.

I would also like to explain what I mean when I use certain terms. I use the term "Indigenous" to include the First Peoples of this land known as Canada today. I use this term because of what I learned from Chief Oren Lyons. In a talk given to Humboldt State University students on Columbus Day in 2010, Chief Lyons explains that in 1975 Indigenous people came together to decide on a name that they wanted to use to name themselves and not continue to use names that settlers created to describe us.[3]

In some of my writing I use the term "Indian." This is always within the context and time frame where this was the common term used. I personally would never use this word to describe Indigenous people outside of this specific context.

I also use the term "historically silenced" a lot in my writing. This, for me, speaks to the voices that have not been included in the education system, such as Indigenous voices, Black voices, and the voices of other groups of people whose cultures, stories, or presence is not included in the education system.

I would also like to bring attention to the acronym "IBPOC" (Indigenous, Black, and People of Colour). This is usually seen as "BIPOC" (Black, Indigenous, and People of Colour), which started in the United States. Recently, in many academic circles and Indigenous communities in Canada, the acronym has changed to focus on the impacts of cultural genocide on the Indigenous peoples of this land. I also focus my writing on Indigenous peoples and the Indigenous experience. Therefore, when I write, I want to be clear that my work and my writing

As educators, the first step we need to take is to unlearn the colonial framework of education.

---

focus on Indigenous peoples. In both acronyms, the reason that Indigenous and Black people are separated out from people of colour is because both groups have been impacted not only by racism and oppression but also by genocide and slavery.

Finally, when I use the word "wholistic," I spell it with the *w* purposefully, because when I am speaking about wholistic education and wholistic learning, I see it as a whole—as in, complete and circular. When I see the word "holistic," I see a hole in the ground, and this is not what I mean when I use this word.

THE WRITING and teaching that I share with you within this book is a product of my many years of supporting Indigenous and non-Indigenous preservice educators, educators, and administrators. It is also a product of my own teacher practice and doctoral work. I have been in many different roles throughout my educational journey, and it seems that I am always in a classroom, either as an educator or as a student. For the past five years, I have been working with preservice educators. This has been the most rewarding work that I have done in my many roles. I think of working with preservice educators as the kindergarten classroom for new teachers. Kindergarteners come in wide-eyed and so excited to be there (well, not all of them), and I feel the same kind of energy from preservice educators. They are so willing and excited to be learning, growing, and becoming change-makers in the system. This kind of energy is powerful to be a part of. Knowing that I am supporting people who will be the next leaders in the classrooms and in districts is a gift that I am so thankful for.

I always ask new educators why they want to be an educator. I hear so often that the reason is they want to be the educator they needed when they were a student, an educator who will see students in their wholeness and support their needs. This is one of the main reasons that keep me in the role of an educator. I want to be the educator that shifts students' thinking about what education can be if we centre the learning on relationships. This style of education would have been a game-changer for me as a student in the K–12 system and even more so now as a PhD student.

The education system in what is known today as Canada is a harmful place for Indigenous students. Every day, Indigenous students feel the effects of racism and oppression in and outside the classroom, in the form of racial slurs or historically incorrect information that perpetuates negative stereotypes of Indigenous peoples. Students are also racially spotlighted within classrooms, being asked to speak for their entire race about topics that they might not know anything about. The list of daily microaggressions and wrong information shared as fact within the education system is endless. The oppression and harm that happens to Indigenous students within educational spaces needs to stop. This book will help educators learn the steps needed to better support Indigenous students within the education system.

I am a believer in the power of education to change lives. Education can support the change needed for all historically silenced students within the system. As educators, the first step we need to take is to unlearn the colonial framework of education. As Marie Battiste discusses in the opening chapter of her book *Decolonizing Education: Nourishing the Learning Spirit*, we as Canadians have been marinated in eurocentrism within our education and we now need to unlearn the way we have been taught, so that we can start to engage in transformational learning spaces.[4] These spaces include many perspectives, many voices, many worldviews, and many ways to engage in the learning process.

Re-Storying the system means that we include the historically silenced voices in education to transform classrooms into spaces of deep learning, relationships, and growth. Within these pages, I share with you my learning from the work that I have been doing in my classrooms, at professional development days, during keynote speeches, and in teacher education classrooms. The hope is for you to find some nuggets of knowledge and practice that you can take with you into your own classroom. Whether you are in the K–12 system, an administrator, or in higher education, there is something here for you. I have been in all these spaces as an educator, administrator, and student, and this work will support you with options to engage at all different levels. This is an invitation for you to reimagine how education unfolds in schools and universities. It will also give you the opportunity to change the single-sided story we have been taught in the western colonial education system.

"Decolonization" is a term that has become more popular within these last few years. I am always thinking about what decolonization means for educators and educational spaces. I know that the system will never be fully decolonized, but I think that it is possible to activate decolonial practices in the classroom to support what has been missing for so many who have come before us.

I am a musician at heart, and music for me has always been a connector. When I teach, I always open my classes with different Indigenous music that connects with the day's learning experiences. I have included that musical element within this book for you as playlists. I also include QR codes that take you to my website for links to the songs. Now, not all the music is by Indigenous artists, and a couple of the items on the playlists are talks, but I have personally selected songs and themes that connect with each chapter. This connection to music is a way to uplift Indigenous voices in music. I hope you enjoy the musical interludes and find new favourite artists within the work. With that being said, my first two offerings to you are "Ah Ni Nah" by Squamish Knowledge Keeper Dennis Joseph and "Remember Me" by Fawn Wood.[5]

1

History

I want to get rid of the Indian problem… Our objective is to continue until there is not a single Indian in Canada that has not been absorbed into the body politic and there is no Indian question, and no Indian Department.

DUNCAN CAMPBELL SCOTT[1]

PLAYLIST

"How Civilization Has Tricked Us All," talk by Dr. Lyla June Johnston at Wisdom 2.0

"Stolen Land," live performance by William Prince and Elisapie Isaac (song by Bruce Cockburn)

"How to Steal a Canoe," music/poem video, by Leanne Betasamosake Simpson

"Sky World," song by Bear Fox, dance performed by Teio Swathe

"Performance for Missing and Murdered Indigenous Women and Girls," live performance with music from A Tribe Called Red

Scan this QR code for links to these videos.

BEFORE WE step into the work of decolonizing education, we need to look back at how we got to where we are today, to fully understand how we can repair the damage done. It is not new information that the Canadian government and education system has been devastatingly harmful for Indigenous people. In fact, starting in 1907, report after report about this very topic has been written in the colonial society of this place known as Canada today. These reports have been explaining, discussing, and educating the government about the harms that have happened and continue to happen to Indigenous people within the education system.

The current public education system in Canada was built by white, colonial, settler society for white, colonial, settler society. The education system that is in place in Canada today was built by one of the key designers of the Indian Residential School System (IRSS)—Egerton Ryerson, the superintendent of education from 1844 to 1876. He is known as the "father of the public education system," and he was responsible for introducing school boards, free elementary education for all, compulsory attendance, and the elementary, high school, and college levels of education. He, along with John A. Macdonald, wrote the blueprint for the IRSS. Ryerson, gathering information from the Bagot Report that addressed industrial schools being the better choice for Indigenous students, created a separate report for Macdonald in 1847 stating that Indigenous students needed to be minimally educated in reading, writing, and math, and that their schooling needed to focus on manual labour training and teaching of religion. Ryerson believed that teaching religion was the only way Indigenous people would be willing to give up their cultural ways. As a part of this report, it was also noted that day schools were not successful, and children needed to be taken out of their home communities to "civilize" them into settler society.[2]

Ryerson brought the model of labour schools to Canada, with the goal of total assimilation. The Indian Residential School System decimated Indigenous languages, separated Indigenous families, and allowed for rampant sexual abuse and harm to happen to children as young as five years old. These places they called "schools" also forcibly indoctrinated Indigenous children into the english language and religion that was not their own. Indian Residential Schools, along with governmental genocidal policies and laws, have destroyed Indigenous families, people, and culture.

This was just one of the many ways the Government of Canada tried to eliminate Indigenous peoples. I think of what the Government of Canada did to destroy Indigenous peoples as a one-thousand-piece puzzle. The IRSS is just one piece of that puzzle. You need each piece of the puzzle to see the whole picture. Learning about the history of colonization on this land and the people of this land is built on those pieces. Some days I feel like I have six hundred to seven hundred pieces of the puzzle and then I listen to something new or a new book comes out, and I find out that I only have about four hundred pieces. The number of pieces to the puzzle I have shifts and changes all the time because I am constantly learning new things and adding to my knowledge.

That is the process of the learning and unlearning journey. Your understanding will always fluctuate, but the goal is to continue to listen, learn, and build understanding. The hope is that change will happen for Indigenous students within the colonial education system, because in this moment, Indigenous peoples are surviving a cultural genocide that continues to happen to them within the current educational system. This chapter will help you see some of the many different ways Indigenous people have been harmed and continue to be harmed by colonization. You can think of it like death by a million paper cuts.

Reports on Indigenous Education in Canada

Part of the history of Indigenous education comes through reports that the government and Indigenous people have written, to show what is needed within the education system for things to get better for Indigenous students and communities. Unfortunately, with every new report, we can see that what the report is asking for sounds very familiar to a report that came before it. Let's take a walk through some of the key reports that have been written over time to better understand some of the issues. Please take note that this is not an extensive list of reports; there are others. These are just a few that I believe are important for education and educators to know about.

Report on the Indian Schools of Manitoba and the Northwest Territories

One of the first official reports about the educational system's failure to support Indigenous students in this place known as Canada today was the *Report on the Indian Schools of Manitoba and the Northwest Territories* of 1907, written by Dr. Peter Bryce, which later became a book called *A National Crime.*[3] Bryce was trained as a doctor and was appointed the chief medical officer of the federal government's Department of Indian Affairs in 1904. Part of Bryce's work was to travel to Indian

Residential Schools in Manitoba and the Northwest Territories. The schools had an extremely high death rate and Bryce was sent by the government to find out why.

Bryce's report told the story of how the residential schools were failing and killing Indigenous students at an alarming rate. He found the schools were underfunded, under-staffed, and that 50 to 70 percent of students who attended the schools were dying. Bryce demanded that Indigenous children deserved a better education and a place where they were safe. He reported that the schools should be either shut down or funded properly. Because his report demanded better for Indigenous children, when Bryce brought it to the government, it was thrown out and he was forced to retire. The government did not want to address the issues at the Indian Residential Schools. To the contrary, in 1920, thirteen years after the report, Duncan Campbell Scott created a law that made it mandatory for all Indigenous children to attend Indian Residential Schools or day schools. If the children did not go to these schools, their parents would be thrown in jail and the children would be taken anyway.

I see the *Report on the Indian Schools of Manitoba and the Northwest Territories* as a key piece in identifying the assimilation process enacted by the Canadian government on Indigenous peoples. The government knew the schools were underfunded and children were dying, but it continued to remove children from Indigenous homes, sending them to places that were detrimental to their well-being and Indigeneity.

Hawthorn Report (*A Survey of the Contemporary Indians of Canada*)

The next report that I believe is important is known as the Hawthorn Report, named for its editor, H.B. Hawthorn. The full name of the report, published in 1966, is *A Survey of the Contemporary Indians of Canada: Economic, Political, Educational Needs and Policies*.[4] This report was requested by the federal Minister of Citizenship and Immigration in 1964. The University of British Columbia was asked to research and compile this report about the social, educational, and economic situation of Indigenous peoples across Canada to determine what support they needed from the government. This research included forty academics consulting with Indigenous peoples and groups across Canada. The report clearly stated that Indigenous peoples in Canada had been marginalized and disadvantaged by the Canadian governmental system, including harm, racism, and genocide from the Indian Residential School System. Within the report, Hawthorn concluded from the research that Indigenous peoples of Canada were "citizens minus" because of their unpreparedness to participate in western society. The Hawthorn Report called for Indigenous peoples to be treated like equal citizens of Canada and be provided with the resources for self-determination. Hawthorn used the term "citizens plus" as a way to address that Indigenous peoples needed to be provided opportunities to be equal citizens in Canadian society. Essentially, the report was saying that Indigenous people would be absorbed into society and lose their land rights. This report started the conversation in government that lead to the White Paper, which I will speak to in the next section.

White Paper of 1969 (Statement of the Government of Canada on Indian Policy)

The White Paper of 1969 was a Canadian policy paper presented to parliament, not a report about Indigenous education, but it substantially influenced a subsequent report called *Indian Control of Indian Education* (discussed below), so it is important to touch on it briefly.

As noted in the resource Indigenous Foundations, "In the Canadian legislature, a policy paper is called a *white paper*. For many First Nations people, the term ironically implies a reference to racial politics and the white majority. The 1969 white paper proposing the abolition of the Indian Act was formally called the Statement of the Government of Canada on Indian Policy."[5] In 1969, Prime Minister Pierre Trudeau and Minister of Indian Affairs Jean Chrétien proposed this legislation that would eliminate Indian Status, which represents Indigenous peoples' lawful rights to their lands. The policy also aimed to convert reserves to fee simple lands, which would give ownership of their reserve lands to Indigenous peoples. It proposed to dissolve Indian Affairs and give jurisdiction of Indigenous peoples to each province to handle in how it saw fit. It would also terminate all treaties across Canada.

Indigenous peoples across Canada responded swiftly and with strength after the news of this paper came out. For the first time in Canada, Indigenous peoples gathered together as one large group to fight back against this law of total assimilation. Two papers were written by Indigenous peoples in retaliation to the White Paper; they were the Red Paper and Wahbung. These papers clearly stated to the Canadian government that it could not get rid of the Indian Act, could not eliminate Indian Status rights and treaty rights, and could not do anything in relation to Indigenous peoples without Indigenous consent. Trudeau and Chrétien withdrew the White Paper in 1970 and the legislation was never passed.

Indian Control of Indian Education

The next demand for change in the lives of Indigenous people in Canada came in the form of a 1972 policy paper titled *Indian Control of Indian Education*.[6] The National Indian Brotherhood, now known today as the Assembly of First Nations, presented this paper to the Minister of Indian Affairs and Northern Development in retaliation to the White Paper of 1969. *Indian Control of Indian Education* is a compilation of papers from Indigenous communities across Canada. It was the first education paper that was written by Indigenous people. It was the first time Indigenous peoples had a say in what they wanted in education for their children. The Brotherhood demanded that the government mandate Indigenous education in all public school systems, including having Indigenous education departments and Indigenous staff. The Brotherhood asked for curriculum and resources that focused on teaching Indigenous history and pedagogy for all schools across this place known as Canada today. To educate all citizens about the Indigenous peoples of this land, including the history of oppression and genocide against Indigenous peoples. The focus of the Brotherhood's work was for Indigenous people to be in charge of educating their own children and for Indigenous communities to have self-sovereignty over teaching their children their language, culture, and traditions.

This short and meaningful policy paper was a roadmap for the changes needed to support Indigenous students in their home communities and to educate the broader public in Canada, within the public education system, about the shared colonial history of this place known as Canada. The paper also called for the system to support non-Indigenous educators in learning about the shared history by making resources available for educators. It proposed placing Indigenous support workers in schools and employing Indigenous educators in the public school system. This paper was written in 1972 demanding self-sovereignty for Indigenous people over their education and it is only recently, more than fifty years later, that First Nations are now gaining jurisdiction over their education systems on reserve.

Royal Commission on Aboriginal Peoples (RCAP) Report

The 1990 Kanesatake Resistance, or what is known as the "Oka Crisis" in colonial terms, was a wake-up call for Canada about Indigenous Peoples' land rights. This seventy-eight-day standoff

My children are the first children in my family who have not been stolen from their parents by the government.

---

between the Kanyen'kehà:ka Mohawk people, the Quebec police, the RCMP, and the Canadian Army occurred when the town of Oka wanted to expand a golf course and put in townhouses onto the traditional lands and burial site of the Kanyen'kehà:ka people. The Kanyen'kehà:ka people had been fighting for their land rights to this piece of land since the 1700s. The Mohawk people were moved to this land from Montreal in 1721 and promised that this land would be considered their land. Since the Mohawk people were not involved in the negotiations of this land, there was conflict. In 1762 Kanesatake was awarded to the Mohawk people. But in 1841 the British recognized the area to belong to the Sulpicians, which the Mohawk people have challenged ever since.[7] In 1989 the mayor of Oka announced the golf course expansion and townhouses on this land, with no consultation with the Kanyen'kehà:ka people. In the summer of 1990 the Kanyen'kehà:ka people created a blockade, not allowing for the developer to move onto their lands, as well as closing down a major highway, so that the government would pay attention to and protect their land rights. Four thousand soldiers of the Canadian Army were brought in to remove the Kanyen'kehà:ka people fighting for their land rights on their own land. The protest ended when the golf course expansion and townhouse project were cancelled, and the federal government purchased the land. The government said it purchased the land to create reserve land, but at the time of this writing, a reserve has yet to be created.

The golf course was never built on the land, and this crisis became one of the most public conflicts for land rights for Indigenous people in Canada.[8] There is a powerful movie about it from the perspective of a young child called *Beans*, directed by Mohawk filmmaker Tracey Deer.[9] I highly recommend watching it and using it as a teaching tool in higher education and high school classrooms.

After the Kanesatake Resistance, in 1991 the Canadian government established the Royal Commission on Aboriginal Peoples (RCAP). This commission was created to investigate, yet again, the relationship between Indigenous people and the Canadian government, and to propose solutions to address the conflicts Indigenous people had with the Canadian government. In 1996, the Commission issued an in-depth report of four thousand pages, addressing the complicated relationships between Indigenous peoples, the western colonial government, and the education system of Canada.[10] The report concluded that drastic changes were needed in the relationships between the Canadian government, the people of Canada, and Indigenous peoples. It called upon the government to take action, with 440 comprehensive recommendations that ranged from creating an Aboriginal Parliament, land rights, education, health care, hunting and fishing rights, and so much more. This report demanded a commitment to new ethical principles in its relationship with the Indigenous peoples of this land. The report provided clear steps and a twenty-year action plan to improve life for Indigenous people and build better relationships between Indigenous peoples and the Canadian government. The Canadian government never fully implemented the majority of the calls to action, and many of the conflicts between the Government of Canada and Indigenous peoples remain unaddressed to this day. Decades later, you might think this report had been written today with the same issues still to be addressed today.

Truth and Reconciliation Commission (TRC) Report

In 2006, the largest class-action settlement in Canada to date, the Indian Residential Schools Settlement Agreement (IRSSA), concluded that the Government of Canada was responsible for the Indian Residential School System (IRSS) and the harms that have happened and continue to happen to the Indigenous peoples of Canada because they were legally mandated to attend the schools.[11] Over 150,000 children were mandated to attend between 1831 and 1997, when the last federally run school closed.[12]

In 2008, a portion of the money from this win was used to push the government to teach the truth about the IRSS and the colonial history of this land by creating the Truth and Reconciliation Commission of Canada (TRC). This commission investigated the IRSS and the history connected to the places they called "schools." The final report of the TRC, published in 2015, is a massive, six-volume set about the history of the residential school system in this place known as Canada. The report was through an Indigenous lens to make sure that this history was recorded and written down, never to be forgotten again. The report includes ninety-four calls to action for the government and people of Canada.[13] These calls to action are clear and workable steps to a better relationship with the Indigenous peoples of this land. Calls numbered six to twelve specifically address education and demand change in the education system, for teaching about the true history of colonization, the IRSS, and the Indigenous peoples of this land.

The education calls also mandate that Indigenous education be a part of all school curriculum, from K–12 to higher education, including a mandatory Indigenous education course for all teacher education programs.

At the time of this writing, only thirteen of the ninety-four calls to action have been implemented, some have been started but not completed, and eighteen have not even been started yet.[14]

Missing and Murdered Indigenous Women and Girls (MMIWG) Report

The latest report from the government is *Reclaiming Power and Place: The Final Report of the National Inquiry into Missing and Murdered Indigenous Women and Girls*, published in 2019.[15] Almost one hundred reports across Canada have been written about the disproportionate violence that continues to happen to Indigenous women and girls. The MMIWG report speaks directly to the systemic racism, colonization, sexism, and discrimination that has created violence toward Indigenous women and girls at epidemic levels. According to the Assembly of First Nations, Indigenous women are four times more likely than non-Indigenous women to be victims of violence.[16]

The National Inquiry into MMIWG comprehensively researched the underlying historical causes and social, institutional, and economic issues that perpetuate oppression, racism, and violence against Indigenous women and girls in Canada. The report highlights how systemic racism, colonialism, and sexism in Canada create unsafe living conditions for Indigenous women and girls, as well as all Indigenous peoples. The report includes 231 calls to action for justice, directed at the government, educational institutions, social service providers, industries, and all Canadians. These demands for change are for safer living conditions and a better life for Indigenous women and girls across this land. When I read this report, it feels like what it is asking for is basic human rights for Indigenous women and girls.

A Turning Point

I would like to circle back and connect to the paper quoted at the welcome into this book: Verna Kirkness and Ray Barnhardt's groundbreaking paper "First Nations and Higher Education: The

Four R's—Respect, Relevance, Reciprocity, Responsibility."[17] Kirkness and Barnhardt, and all of the above-mentioned reports, have been asking for a better education system that teaches about, sees, and honours the Indigenous peoples of this land.

We are at a turning point with Indigenous children. I see it from my own lived experience with my own children and from watching how children in my community are now learning and being grounded in their language and culture at such a young age. My children are the first children in my family who have not been stolen from their parents by the government. This turning point means that my children now have an opportunity to be connected to their Indigenous culture and family from birth. This is a huge moment for my family. This turning point from my personal perspective is that my children have a better understanding of colonization, Indigenous peoples, race, and racism. They are so knowledgeable at such a young age and can speak to it, address it, and teach others about it. Had I had this information when I was young, I would have been a force. I see in my children that they have a stronger voice and feel more confident in challenging the misinformation being taught and addressing the colonial violence that happens in schools every day. My heart fills with pride knowing that my children have a better chance at living with less intergenerational trauma and disconnection from who they are as Indigenous people than I did.

Laws

Since the beginning of colonial Canada, many policies and laws of the Canadian government have harmed Indigenous people by using colonialism, assimilation, a western colonial education system, and systemic racism as tools of genocide to eliminate Indigenous people and remove them from their lands. This last point is a critical aspect of colonization, because everything that Indigenous people have endured and continue to endure to this day is directly tied to the dispossessions of their lands. Here, I will cover, in brief, the Royal Proclamation of 1763 and the Indian Act.

The Royal Proclamation of 1763

Issued by King George III, British parliament, the Royal Proclamation of 1763[18] marks a pivotal moment for Indigenous people in Canada and the British Crown. The Royal Proclamation recognizes Indigenous people as Nations/tribes and that they owned the land, and established an administrative structure, protocols, and rules of engagement with Indigenous peoples in the treaty-making process in Canada. It affirms the first major principle of British/Indigenous policy: that Indigenous peoples on their Indigenous lands were to be protected from unscrupulous land speculators and traders. The proclamation explicitly states that Indigenous peoples have the rights and titles to their land until ceded only to the British Crown. This document forbid settlers from claiming Indigenous lands without treaties or purchase.

The land cession and treaty system of present-day Ontario and western Canada can be traced back to the Royal Proclamation. The proclamation was the starting point of how the land of Canada was to be acquired, and the protocols were in place as a way to ensure that the Indigenous peoples were a part of the treaty-making process. Considering this document and British Columbia, my thoughts then go to, "How was it that the land we are on today, unceded territory, was then stolen from Indigenous peoples?" The proclamation was also a pivotal piece for the most important land title case in Canadian history, *Delgamuukw v. British Columbia*.[19] This win stated that Indigenous peoples held property rights to their lands as a collective Nation; it also included oral stories into the process of establishing land rights.

Under the Indian Act, First Nations were prevented from using the system of law in place to defend their rights to their own lands.

This opened the door to all other Nations with their fight for the rights to their lands since time out of mind.

The Royal Proclamation is still an important document, and no law has ever disputed it. Section 25 of the *Constitution Act, 1982*, included the Royal Proclamation and legally recognized Indigenous land rights.

The Indian Act

In 1876, not long after Canadian Confederation in 1867, the Indian Act was implemented into Canadian law, to control Indigenous people, and it continues to this day to control the lives of Indigenous peoples in Canada.[20] Although I highlight some key points about the Act below, I cannot cover everything about it within this book. There are many other places that you can find more information. I highly recommend Bob Joseph's *21 Things You Might Not Know about the Indian Act* as a great starting place for learning more about how the Indian Act was designed to assimilate and eliminate Indigenous peoples of Canada.[21]

Reserves. Reserves are land parcels that the Canadian government holds in trust for Indigenous communities. These lands are managed by the government under the Indian Act and are a fraction of the land that Indigenous people had prior to contact.[22] These lands were made to make Indigenous people settle in one location. This was not something that Indigenous communities would do—their lives were dependent on food sources and they chose locations that were better places to live off the land each season. Under colonial rule, Indigenous communities were told to up and leave locations that were rich in food sources and close to waterways, like Seṅáḵw. Seṅáḵw was a Squamish Nation village site that is known colonially today as Vanier Park in Vancouver. In 1913, the land where the Seṅáḵw village was, was in high demand from settlers. So, the government brought a barge to the shore, and the Indian agent told the Squamish village residents that they needed to pack up their homes and get on the barge. Once everyone was off the land, the barge was sent out to sea. The village was burned to the ground and the people were adrift. Luckily the owner of a tugboat operation saw the barge adrift and pulled it to where the Squamish Nation's Capilano reserve is today, in North Vancouver.[23]

Reserve lands are not owned by the Indigenous peoples that live there. Under Canadian law, the land is owned by the Crown. This means that people who live on this land cannot sell the land, mortgage the land, or use it for collateral on loans.

Status cards. The Indian Act is governed through the federal government of Canada. Through this act, it controls and determines who is and who is not "Indian" under the lens of Canadian law with status cards—and we still have these cards today. In this section I will be using the term "Indian" because within the Act this is the term used to discuss this topic. Note that status cards are not used for Inuit and Métis people, who are also Indigenous to the land known as Canada today. This is a bigger conversation about the Indigenous people of Canada that I won't be able to discuss in this book but will maybe do so at a future date in another book. I encourage you to learn more about this topic; you can find out more in the Royal Commission on Aboriginal Peoples Report.[24]

A very important part of having a status card for Indigenous people is that the status card connects Indigenous people to community and most importantly connects them to treaty and land rights. In the colonial mindset, Indian Status is determined by how much "Indian blood" a person has—a system very much like one used for dogs and horses. Let's take a pause here to think about that and let that sink in for a moment.

This concept of "Indian blood" was created by white settlers to measure the "amount" of Indian blood a person has, and it controls who is allowed to be Indian and who is not allowed to be Indian in the eyes of Canadian law. It was intended as a way to eliminate Indigenous people over time. The more "diluted" a person's "Indian blood" is considered, the less and less Indian they become under Canadian law. For example, in colonial terms, the government uses numbers to identify who is Indian; they use 6(1) and 6(2) to describe Indian blood. These numbers are in reference to the sections of the Indian Act. These two sections describe how the law identifies Indian people. To simplify these numbers, 6(1) would be considered "full status": this means that the person considered to be Indian can pass on Indian Status to their children. 6(2) would be considered mixed race Indian, one parent 6(1) and another parent non-Indian under the law. If two "full-status" 6(1) Indians have a baby, the baby is considered "full status," or 6(1). If one parent is non-Indian under the law and the other "full-status" Indian, their child is considered mixed race, or 6(2). The mixed-race child still has Indian Status, but if the mixed child has a child with a non-Indian person under the law, then that child will not have status. The hope with this law was to slowly eliminate the perceived "Indian problem," as Duncan Campbell Scott said. If there are no Indian people on the land, then there can be no land claims and the land would be free and clear to use as the government wants to.

I would like to point out this is a very complicated process that has multiple variables that are used to define Indian blood. The process was meant to be complicated. Please find out more information on the government website[25] and Indigenous Foundations website.[26] The hope was always to eliminate Indigenous people after two generations.

See the following illustration that shows how this colonial system of measurement works with my own family.

How Indian Status Works in My Family

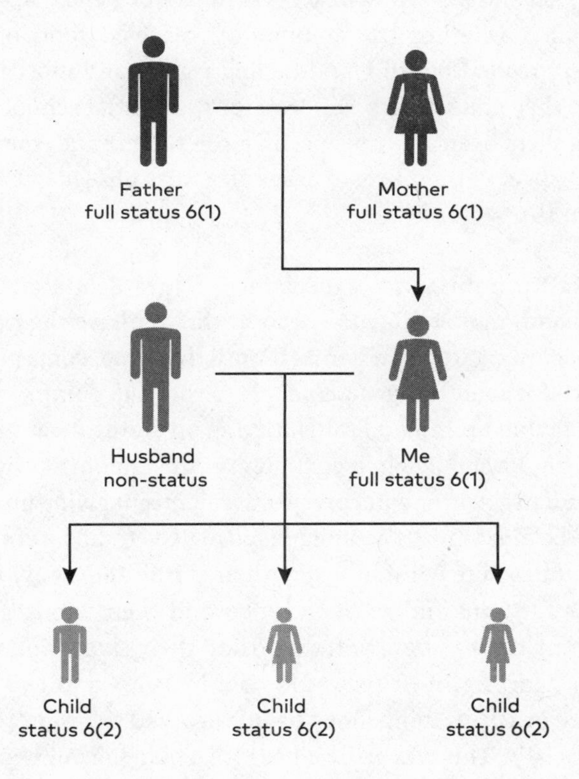

Under the Indian Act, in order for my children to pass on Indian Status to their children, they will need to have children with either a 6(1) or 6(2) Indian Status to pass on their status. If they have children with a non-status person, then my grand-children will not have Indian Status under Canadian law.

Indian agents. The Indian agent was a male person who worked for the government to supervise and control Indigenous people on reserves. These agents were mandated to enforce the Indian Act and were the gatekeepers for coming and going: they controlled whether the community received food or not; they controlled hunting and fishing rights; and most importantly, they collected up children for residential schools. The Indian agent oversaw all people living on reserve and controlled every aspect of their lives. These roles were phased out, beginning in 1960.

Voting. Up until 1949, except for in Nova Scotia and Newfoundland, most Indigenous people did not have the right to vote according to the Indian Act. Until that time, some policies allowed for some Indigenous people to vote, but doing so would mean giving up Indian Status. Giving up status meant losing treaty rights and living in community. Most importantly, from a Canadian governmental perspective, it meant giving up rights to land claims. In 1924, Indigenous male veterans were given the right to vote without losing their status and treaty rights. In 1944, Status Indian servicemen and their spouses were given the right to vote without losing their status and treaty rights. Starting in British Columbia in 1949 and ending in Quebec in 1969, Indigenous peoples gained the right to vote provincially. This was critical because a person could not vote federally if they were not allowed to vote provincially. In 1950, Inuit were given the right to vote federally but because they were in remote locations, they did not have access to polling stations. It was not until 1960 that Indigenous people could vote in federal elections without having to give up their status and treaty rights.

Some interesting history about voting prior to 1960 is that in the mid-1880s Indigenous men were given the right to vote, because the government in charge believed that if they gave them the right to vote, that the Indigenous people would vote for them. This did not happen. Then the people in charge changed the law saying that only civilized male people had the right to vote, but under the law Indigenous people were not "persons" so they lost their right to vote.[27]

Enfranchisement. In 1880, the Government of Canada amended the Indian Act to stipulate that if an Indigenous person was certified as a lawyer, doctor, or educator, they would be automatically enfranchised, which meant losing Indian Status and connections to land rights and treaty rights. An enfranchised person was no longer considered an Indian under governmental law. Enfranchised people were removed from reserves—cut off from their home, community, and family. One intention of this law was to deny more Indigenous people of their land claim rights, but it was also used to remove Indigenous people from their culture and community and stop them from working for the betterment of Indigenous peoples. This law was in place until 1951.

Hunting and fishing rights. In 1880, another amendment to the Indian Act was to regulate Indigenous peoples' rights to hunt and fish. The Act controlled when and where Indigenous peoples could hunt and fish and forbade them from hunting and fishing for commercial purposes. The purpose behind this was to control and cut off Indigenous peoples' ability to provide for their communities and families: If people are dependent on you for their livelihood, then you can control them.

Indigenous people continue to fight for hunting and fishing rights today. For example, a landmark court case from the Supreme Court of Canada decided in 1999 that the Mi'kmaq community in Nova Scotia has the right to a "moderate livelihood." The case was won because of the wording in the Peace and Friendship Treaty that was signed in 1752, stating that the Indigenous people "shall not be hindered from, but have free liberty of hunting and fishing as usual."[28] This case recognized Indigenous rights to fishing. But Indigenous people today in Mi'kmaq territories are still fighting non-Indigenous people for their right to fish. This is highlighted in the current-day lobster dispute in 2020 between the Sipekne'katik First Nation and non-Indigenous fishermen in Nova Scotia.[29] I encourage you to learn more about this.

The pass system. This was a governmental system that was put in place from 1885 to the 1940s to control the movement of Indigenous people living on reserves. It was put in place around the time of the North-West Resistance and was intended as a temporary policy to keep Indigenous people on reserves and unable to fight. The Indian agent attached to a reserve had the power to say if the people living on reserve were allowed to leave or not. If an Indigenous person wanted to leave the reserve for hunting, fishing, or visiting family on other reserves, they had to ask permission from the Indian agent. The agent would either give or not give the Indigenous person a pass. The pass would state where and when the Indigenous person was allowed to be. If an Indigenous person was found off reserve without a pass, they would be thrown in jail. If they were found somewhere that was not on the pass, they would be thrown in jail. This tool was in place for almost sixty years.

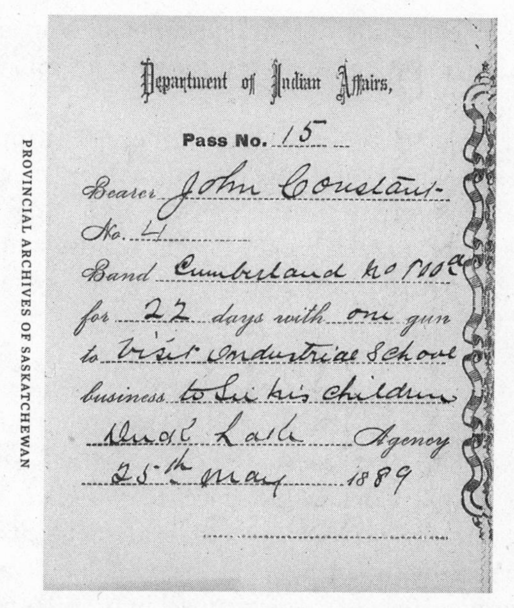
Department of Indian Affairs,

Pass No. 15

Bearer John Constant

No. 4

Band Cumberland No 100

for 22 days with one gun

to visit Industrial School

business to see his children

Duck Lake Agency

25th May 1889

PROVINCIAL ARCHIVES OF SASKATCHEWAN

A pass giving the bearer permission to visit his children.

Indian conspiracy laws. These laws were put in place to stop Indigenous people from fighting back against the Canadian government and their laws. Among the first of these laws were those that made it illegal for Indigenous people to practise their culture and ceremonies, for example, the Potlatch and Sundance ban from 1885 to 1951. These traditional practices, from time out of mind, are ceremonies where Indigenous peoples gather together and celebrate who they are, and pass down language, dances, stories, traditions, and laws.

The government also wanted Indigenous people to adopt the western colonial mindset of living, so banning the Potlatch and Sundance was also a way to destroy Indigenous culture. During a Potlatch you could have up to two thousand or more people gathered from all up and down the West Coast. When

Indigenous people gathered, the government worried they would make plans to combat against the government and colonial laws.

Another one of the conspiracy laws made it illegal for Indigenous people to gather in groups of more than three people while off reserve from 1927 to 1951. It was also against the law for Indigenous people to raise money to fight against land claims, or anything that was in the Indian Act in the court system, also from 1927 to 1951.[30]

Residential schools. A main policy of the Indian Act was to assimilate Indigenous people into the "body politic." One of the ways this was done was through the creation of Indian Residential Schools, a system that we have touched on already. Duncan Campbell Scott, who was seventeen when he got his first job as a copy clerk in the Department of Indian Affairs, became the deputy superintendent of the department in 1913. He held that post until 1932, overseeing and enforcing the Indian Act and creating policies and laws that were detrimental to Indigenous people. In 1920, Scott created a law that made it mandatory for Indigenous children to attend Indian Residential Schools, as well as expanding the IRSS. He held his position in Indian Affairs for longer than anyone else who has held this role, and under his direction more than four thousand children died in the residential school system.[31]

Ban on raising money for legal matters. In 1927, the Indian Act was amended to make it illegal for anyone, Indigenous people or non-Indigenous people, to solicit funds for legal fights for land rights, hunting rights, and fishing rights, effectively preventing any Indigenous person or community from using the system of law in place to defend their rights to their lands and provide for their communities. This was in effect until 1951.

Peasant farming laws. Once Indigenous people were forced to farm like europeans did, they did it in ways that connected to the land, and they were excellent at farming. To slow down Indigenous farmers, another amendment from 1880 made it illegal under the Indian Act for Indigenous people to sell farmed goods and food. The peasant farming laws dictated that Indigenous people could not use machines in their farming; they could only use hand tools to farm. Indigenous people also had to ask the government permission to sell their produce to not be in competition with settler farmers.[32] Knowing this is just an entry point into learning this history, I encourage you to continue to read, listen, and learn more about these laws.

Laws in the Big Picture

I had the opportunity to see Murray Sinclair when he visited UBC a few years back; his words and viewpoint helped me understand things in a big picture way. He connected history with laws.[33] If you were subject to a law today that was unjust or racist, you might hire a lawyer and go to court to fight it. But imagine if the government made it illegal for you to hire a lawyer. You then might say, "Well, okay, I will go to school and become a lawyer so that I can fight this fight myself." And then the government put a law in place that said, "If you become a lawyer, you will no longer be considered a member of your community and so, by this other law, you cannot fight for their rights." At this point you might be furious and want to gather your family and community together to protest these unjust laws. But the government saw that you were going to do this and they created another law that made it illegal for you to gather with more than three of your community members. If you did, you would be arrested and thrown in jail. What options would you have then? You might think the only thing left to do would be to go to war.

Every time Indigenous peoples of this land tried to follow colonial laws, so that they could protect themselves and their children, the government would intentionally and purposefully construct new barriers.

Even considering only a small portion of laws under the Indian Act, we can clearly see that the Canadian government was strategic and methodical about how it treated Indigenous peoples here in this place known as Canada today. Indigenous peoples were not meant to survive and thrive.

Questions for Reflection

- Reflect on the information that you were taught about Indigenous peoples and cultures in your own schooling. What did you learn? What was left out of your education? How does this shape your understanding of Indigenous people today?
- What of the information covered in this chapter did you *not* know before reading it?
- How might you learn more of the missing pieces of the puzzle that makes up the colonial history of this place known as Canada today?
- What are you still wondering about and what do you want to learn more about? What are some ways for you to learn more?
- How does knowing this information support you in your teaching or administrative practice?

Resources

Akiwenzie-Damm, Kateri, et al. *This Place: 150 Years Retold*. Winnipeg, MB: Portage & Main Press, 2019.

CBC Radio. *Secret Life of Canada*. Podcast. https://www.cbc.ca/listen/cbc-podcasts/203-the-secret-life-of-canada.

CBC Radio. *This Place: 150 Years Retold*. Podcast. https://www.cbc.ca/listen/cbc-podcasts/1020-this-place.

Claxton, Nick XEMŦOLTW̱, et al. "Challenging Racist 'British Columbia': 150 Years and Counting." Joint publication of Asian Canadians on Vancouver Island: Race, Indigeneity, and the Transpacific (ACVI) [University of Victoria] and the Canadian Centre for Policy Alternatives (BC Office). February 25, 2021. Available from https://policyalternatives.ca/challengingracistbc.

First Nations and Indigenous Studies. "Reserves." Indigenous Foundations, First Nations and Indigenous Studies, University of British Columbia, 2009. https://indigenousfoundations.arts.ubc.ca/reserves/.

Gray, Lynda. *First Nations 101: Tons of Stuff You Need to Know*. Updated and expanded 2nd edition. Vancouver: Adaawx Publishing, 2022.

Indian Act (R.S.C., 1985, c. I-5). http://laws-lois.justice.gc.ca/eng/acts/i-5/.

Joseph, Bob. *21 Things You Might Not Know about the Indian Act: Helping Canadians Make Reconciliation with Indigenous Peoples a Reality*. Port Coquitlam, BC: Indigenous Relations Press, 2018.

Manuel, Arthur, and Grand Chief Ronald M. Derrickson. *Unsettling Canada: A National Wake-Up Call*. Toronto: Between the Lines, 2021.

Vowel, Chelsea. *Indigenous Writes: A Guide to First Nations, Métis & Inuit Issues in Canada*. Winnipeg, MB: HighWater Press, 2016.

2

Journey through Education

[Indigenous] students experience [our current system of] education as assimilation and nullification of their own identity.

MICHAEL MARKER[1]

PLAYLIST

"Nomads," music video by Aysanabee

"Submerged," video of performance by Kimmortal

"I Can't Remember My Name," music video by Snotty Nose Rez Kids

"Gentle Warrior," music video, song by students and staff at Allison Bernard Memorial High School in Eskasoni, Cape Breton, performed by Kalolin Johnson, featuring Devon Paul and Thunder Herney

"Song of Survival," music video, song by Red Eagle

Scan this QR code for links to these videos.

IN THIS CHAPTER I share with you some of the experiences Indigenous students face in the colonial system. The hope is that this will allow you to see the education system through the lens of students who the system was not made for, and the harms that happen within education for non-white students. It can be difficult to see the system as harmful if you have not been harmed by it, but once you start to see it, you won't be able to unsee it.

As a child of the Sixties Scoop, I was stolen from my home community and family. This started my journey in such a way that I could not fully understand how harmful the school system was for me while I was in it. Now, as an adult looking back, I can see the places where my education put me at a disadvantage, marginalized me, and repeatedly told me that I was not smart enough to be there.

The Lord's Prayer and "O Canada"

Some of my earliest memories of education are standing beside my desk every morning and reciting the Lord's Prayer and singing "O Canada." Looking back now, I can see how this practice reinforced the white colonial narrative that we were to be learning in school. Reciting and singing them both every day, I knew every word—and that was all they were for me, words.

No one explained why we were saying them at the start of each day, but the importance of the work being done was clear: Every child had to learn the words to the prayer and the anthem. I remember standing beside my desk and thinking, in the younger grades, about the words being said in the Lord's Prayer. I was terrified by what "deliver us from evil" meant. Would we be taken away in the night to a graveyard where the evil lives? No idea why I connected the line to a graveyard, but I always thought of it that way when saying it. Starting each day in this space of unease was always something that stood out for me as a child. I am pretty sure I can tell you all the words still, to this day.

This example typifies how the colonial system is set up: students are to be followers without context. This is the core of assimilation, having students repeat chosen words, say what is expected, and forcing and reinforcing it upon all students.

Are there practices you can think of, done in school today, that remind you of this?

In Front of the *Whole* Class

Another vivid memory I have is from grade 3. We were learning about the provinces and territories of Canada. I remember sitting on the floor with all my classmates and the teacher standing above us, holding our tests. She told the class that only one person got a perfect mark on the test, and that she was so surprised at who it was. Then she looked at me and handed me my test back. I did not know how to feel in that moment. I felt good that I did well, but the back-handed compliment shook me to my core. Why did the teacher think I was not going to do well on the test? What other things did my teacher not think I was capable of? Did she not think I was an intelligent student? Even if she did feel that I was not the smartest child in the room, her verbalizing to me and the *whole* class that she didn't think I was smart enough to get 100 percent was damaging to me.

This comment reflected deficit thinking, and this kind of thinking is often connected to Indigenous students in the school system. By saying this to me, the teacher showed that she viewed me as incapable of doing well and that she had low expectations of me and my learning.

The point? What we say to children *matters* and how we see them in the classroom *matters*. If we show students that we believe in them and see them, then they will see and feel that. Students will also see and feel if you do not believe in them, and that contributes to how they think about themselves. This moment contributed to my lack of confidence as a student in the education system and my ability to see myself as smart.

As a student, did you ever feel that an educator set low expectations for you? That they did not think you were smart?

Being Taken Out of Class

In elementary school I was often removed from the classroom and brought to the learning centre. This space is where there were fewer students, and I would have one-on-one time with a teacher to support my reading and writing. In each grade, I was always in the lowest reading group, the smallest reading group, and part of this process was to shuttle me from the larger class to a room with other students who had challenges reading and writing from all grades. This was detrimental to me as a learner. Being pulled out of class because of my low reading skills added to my believing that I was not smart, and it connected to my teacher's low expectations of me as a student. This affected the narrative I told myself, about myself as a student. Being pulled out of class also impacted me socially. It disconnected me from the classroom community and made it challenging for me to form friendships and feel like I was part of the class.

Finally, in grade 7, when I was trying to be more confident, I got up the nerve to ask my teacher to place me in a higher-level reading group. I promised him that I would try really hard to be better. I practised over and over again how I would ask and how I would show him I could do it. I felt like all I needed was a chance to prove to him how good I could be. He didn't even consider it; he couldn't see how I wanted so desperately to be given the opportunity to do better and belong to the larger class. His words back to me were, "I don't think you will be able to do the higher reading level. It will be too hard for you." I was shut down and continued to be pulled out of class, and now I was also the only person in my reading group.

Belonging at school is so important for students. Feeling like an outsider and not part of a group creates isolation. If, in addition to this, certain students don't see any positive representations of their culture or community backgrounds (for example, if only white culture is represented in curriculum, practices, and staffing), how are students supposed to feel like a part of the school? And how well are they set up to do well in school? If a student does not see themselves in the curriculum and the stories in school, they see this as a nullification of their own identity. More on this below.

In what ways can you make sure that you are doing all you can to build a community of belonging in your classroom for all students?

The Importance of Language

Not long after I asked my seventh-grade teacher to change my reading group, I heard a news story about Indigenous children on the radio that hit me to my core being. My dad always listened to CBC Radio in the car and at home. I can still hear all the music transitions from one show to another in the eighties that can bring me back to the family dinner table in an instant. One day when we were in the car, a CBC news report talked about how Indigenous students were failing and dropping out of school at a much higher rate than all other students in the school system.

The impact of this news story on me was detrimental. In this moment, I started thinking that I was not a good student because I was Indigenous. Indigenous students were not good at school, and this was why I could not get into a higher reading group and why my grade 7 teacher was thinking about failing me. It made me believe that because I was Indigenous, I could not be successful. This was also connected to me being in a family of all white people, and in that moment, it was made abundantly clear to me that I would never be as successful or as smart as my family, and I would just have to deal with failure because Indigenous children were not smart.

Looking back on your own education, how often do you remember seeing yourself reflected in the work you were doing? How do you think that impacted you as a student?

This brings to light the importance of language.

The language we use in classrooms, with and about students, has the power to lift students up. But words can also damage students and their spirit. No one deserves to be devalued in educational spaces. Educators in classrooms with diverse students need to take the time to reflect on and educate themselves about the multilayered experiences students come into the classroom with, so that they can see the students in their wholeness. This wholeness includes but is not limited to their culture, their home language, their religion, their gender identity, and their racial identity. Each student that comes into the classroom is a knowledge holder of their own lived experience, and that needs to be honoured.

At this point in my education, I had no idea what it meant to be Indigenous. With no cultural supports in the schools back in those days, I had no cultural support in who I was or anyone to look to, to help me see what being Indigenous meant and that I could be proud of being Indigenous. There was no one around me that could help me sort through who I was and connect me with my Indigenous culture. I just knew that it meant that I was not meant to complete school. My teachers had low expectations of me and little to no faith in my academic success. This continued to be my narrative for so many years. Those teachers shaped who I thought I was: an unsuccessful student who constantly struggled in school.

Sadly, I learned what most of us learned about Indigenous people in education in this time: Indigenous people wore feather headdresses and loin cloths and rode horses, and they helped the settlers settle. There was trading of fur and then some fighting with Louis Riel. And this was all the "Indigenous education" I received in school.

Can you think of moments within your own schooling where the language from the teacher impacted you and your learning?

Representation in Curriculum

What I needed back in school was a way to see myself through the work we did. I needed the curriculum to reflect Indigenous people, history, and culture. This would have allowed me the opportunity to understand who I was and the history of my ancestors on this land. I needed the research that Gloria

Ladson-Billings was working on and developing. Ladson-Billings coined the term "culturally relevant teaching" in 1994; this work is based on teaching that reflects, honours, and recognizes all students in the class and not just the white colonial narrative that has historically been taught. Research has found that non-white students did better in classrooms that represented them in the curriculum, in the books, and in the teaching. This brings us to books that are still being used in classrooms today.

In my grade 8 year in high school, I read *The Outsiders* by S.E. Hinton, like almost everyone from my age group did. The novel was published in 1967. In my day, the movie had just come out and it was all the rage! It was 1983, forty years ago. I was so in love with C. Thomas Howell and the story of the bad boys from the wrong side of the tracks. We also read George Orwell's *Animal Farm*, which was published in 1945.

Recently, all three of my children have read *The Outsiders* and *Animal Farm* in their grade 8 and 10 classrooms. Forty years later and teachers are still using the same books that were written sixty to eighty years ago now. How is the education system changing and reflecting the moment we are in when my children are getting the same lessons and books from my childhood? The world has shifted drastically since these books were written. In educational spaces today, we need to be talking about oppression, racism, identities, and LGBTQ2S+ experiences. These were not topics that we talked about or were taught when I was in school. Also, when I was a student in the K–12 system, we were never asked to use critical thinking about what we were being taught. We were only taught to be consumers of what they delivered to us.

Hinton was fifteen when she started to write *The Outsiders*, and she sold it when she was seventeen. As Margaret Eby writes about Hinton, "Most of the literature handed down for high school students to read had, in Hinton's estimation, nothing to

Always ask: How does this story support students in learning about themselves and the society that they live in?

do with the lived experiences of teenagers in her hometown of Tulsa, Oklahoma."[2] What I find most interesting about Hinton is that she was critical that no one was writing about real topics for young adults at the time. There was not even a genre of young adult books. So, as a middle-class white girl, she wrote an "outsider" story about boys and gangs. She wrote the book because she wanted her education to reflect the world she lived in. The story she wrote was about her viewpoint of the city and the kids that she lived with.

This book has a place in the history of books; it created pathways for authors to write differently for young adults. Hinton forged a space for authors to be real in their writing without watering down stories for younger readers. My experience with students is that they are so much smarter than we give them credit for. I would like to apply what Hinton was doing in that moment in time to today in our current-day classrooms. Hinton wanted her schooling to represent her and her lived experience. She challenged what was being written for young readers, and she wrote about topics that directly impacted her in the place where she lived. She wanted to be able to see herself in what she was reading in school. This is what all schools should be pushing for, a reflection of all students in their classrooms.

Using Curriculum to Rethink What We Teach

The curriculum for grade 10 English in British Columbia, as an example, gives us reason to rethink the stories we teach. The curriculum competencies state:

- Construct meaningful personal connections between self, text, and world.
- Explore how language constructs personal and cultural identities.
- Access information for diverse purposes and from a variety of sources to inform writing.[3]

The first point speaks to the importance of using texts that reflect all students in the classroom; the second speaks to looking at the world through multiple worldviews; and the third speaks to including topics of oppression, racism, Indigenous peoples, white supremacy, and colonialism.

As set out in the BC curriculum, these are the big ideas for grade 10 English:

- The exploration of text and story deepens our understanding of diverse, complex ideas about identity, others, and the world.
- Texts are socially, culturally, geographically, and historically constructed.[4]

These points speak to the need for multiple explorations of non-white authors, stories, and perspectives within the classroom. They also speak directly to the need to teach about the social construct of race and identity, as they are defined in western colonial society and others. They also address the need to teach about the history and land students live on from multiple perspectives.

The history of education in Canada has silenced non-white voices and avoided difficult topics in the curriculum. This has allowed oppression, racism, and harm to happen in classrooms. Educators should be pushing for change by using books and curriculum that reflect the lived experiences of all students in our classrooms. As educators and agents of change, we need to bring in books written by multiple different authors who identify as Indigenous, Black, People of Colour (IBPOC), (dis)abled, LGBTQ2S+, and other equity seeking groups that reflect the challenges students face in today's society. This will support and prepare all students for living in a multicultural society. If we do not allow for students to learn and talk about these topics, then we are doing a disservice to the next generation.

Conversations about Representation

I'd like to share with you some comments and questions that I have received about representation in the classroom and my responses, in hopes to help folks talk through comments when they hear them.

"Well, we need to teach to the white students too."

My response: We have had over 150 years of teaching only to the white students in the classroom. So many children experience education in this system that does not reflect them or share their culture or identity, or even talk about them in a good way. The system has a responsibility to Indigenous students, Black students, and students of colour, just as it does to white students, to learn about and read more than just white stories in education. We also need to be doing the work of uplifting Indigenous brilliance, Black brilliance, and people of colour brilliance in classrooms, talking about more than IBPOC trauma that has been inflicted on us by colonization, so that all students can learn about and understand the peoples whose land they live upon. More on this in chapter 6.

"I didn't find Animal Farm *offensive when I read it in grade 12."*

This comment came from a white, middle-aged male educator. To me, it shows a lack of awareness of the social justice lens that is needed in classrooms today. In social justice work, the most important thing you must be willing to do is to *listen*. To listen to those who have been historically silenced and make sure you are personally doing better for the next generation. If you listen to these voices, you will hear that not having a space in education that represents them as human beings is detrimental to IBPOC students. It also is a major factor in pushing them out of the education system altogether.

This comment showed that the teacher had likely not read *Animal Farm* in the last twenty-plus years and did not understand the book in today's context of education. If he had read the book and had some solid reasoning for teaching it to a class of 95 percent Black and Brown students, then I could have engaged in a conversation about why I think *Animal Farm* is problematic for such a group of students.

The primary reason is that if, as educators, we want to create culturally responsive classrooms, we need to find books, curriculum, and stories that the students in our classrooms can connect to and see themselves reflected in. The education system has focused on european history (*Animal Farm* included) for more than 150 years, while not focusing on the many other voices in the history of this place known as Canada today. *Animal Farm* was written more than seventy-five years ago and has been used in education for the same amount of time. With the help of the internet, students don't even need to read the book. All the answers to the tests, chapter notes, and lesson plans exist online. Even though students have been doing this for some time, teachers don't change what they teach.

My questions to educators who use this book are, How is the Russian Revolution connected to the students in your classroom? How does this story provide relevant information that can support students in learning about themselves and the society that they live in today? Can your students see themselves within the story or characters?

Students need to have windows and mirrors—windows to learn about other perspectives, cultures, and history that has been silenced, and mirrors to see themselves within what they are learning. In recent years, so many excellent books have been written that can connect students to the society they live in, to historically silenced voices, and to all the things that have been eliminated from our education system. That is where educators should focus the learning.

"If we bring in Indigenous books like Monkey Beach *or the Trickster series, parents will push back against the Indigenous content and drugs and alcohol."*

This was said by a principal of a high school when I came in to make a complaint about *Animal Farm*. When saying this, they were clearly not afraid of the pushback from an Indigenous parent about the white author's book that also had drugs and alcohol in it. If the concern with books like *Monkey Beach* by Eden Robinson is that the book talks about drugs and drug abuse, then I have to say: If we are not talking about drugs and drug abuse, then we are not teaching about them. All high school students should be learning about this. There are drug dealers in high schools; drug abuse is happening in real time today, for young adults from all communities, and we have a responsibility to teach about it. We need a curriculum that reflects life for young people today to help them navigate today's society.

For real change to happen for the next generation, we need to provide a well-rounded education that addresses systemic racism, oppression, and the daily impacts of colonialism. If we use outdated materials, lesson plans, and books, we are doing a disservice to all students. If IBPOC students do not see themselves within the curriculum and books, then they feel unseen, unwelcome, and unsafe in educational spaces. If white students never hear the stories of oppression, racism, and harm that happens to IBPOC students, then they will never understand how harmful it is and how they might be participating in the continuation of the oppression and harm.

If we don't change it up, then systemic racism and oppression will just continue the daily harm on all IBPOC students in the education system and in society; it impacts every single one of us, every single day.

Racism/Racial Spotlighting

I know from my own teacher education program that there are many teachers in the system today who were never taught how to address racism in the classroom or how to support a class when something racist happens. This continues the harm for students who experience racism on a daily basis in school settings.

Sometimes, when a racist incident happens, educators ask the student who has been harmed to teach the class about the racism. This practice functions as a form of "racial spotlighting." Dorinda Carter Andrews and her colleagues define racial spotlighting as putting a student in the position of being a token spokesperson for their entire race; often the student will be singled out as the point person on all things that have to do with their race or ethnicity.[5] It also usually happens in real time in a classroom, where students are put on the spot in the moment to answer questions about their entire race. As Carter Andrews et al. go on to explain, this practice, whether well-meaning or not, functions as a "racial microaggression": highlighting a student's minority race status, making them uncomfortable, silent, and even worried that they will be called upon to answer things they might not know anything about. This is unsettling for students and could make them either not want to come to class, not want to participate, or withdraw from the class altogether.

Sadly, this is something that happens regularly for me as a PhD student in higher education. An example of a similar experience for me happened when one of my professors emailed me an invitation to lead one of the classes I was in as a student; it wasn't in front of the whole class, but it was a direct request to be the knowledge holder of all things Indigenous. The class fell on Orange Shirt Day, and the request was for me to share with the class (made up mostly of white students) my knowledge, worldview, teachings, and insight about this day. Because I was in the class as a student, not a teacher, I did not feel like it was my place to do a lesson on the reasons for and importance of Orange Shirt Day. My response to the professor's invitation was that I did not want to lead the class and that it was important for them as the professor/instructor to lead this critical discussion. To help them with their planning, I sent them some literature to read in hopes to deepen their understandings of Orange Shirt Day.

The professor responded by stating that we were all learners and teachers in that space, and we all had something to share. But I did not see other students in the class being asked to teach about their culture or history, so I was curious about why I was being asked to do this work. (I did ask the one other Indigenous student in the class if they had been approached to do this, but they had not.) As a student, I once again had to speak back against the power imbalance in the context of this racial spotlighting. I reminded the professor that I was a student, and I was not interested in taking any kind of leadership role with Indigenous education in the class.

Students should not be asked to be the teachers of all things to do with their race. Spotlighting students in the classroom is putting an unfair responsibility on their shoulders to be the authority of all things to do with their race and the cultures associated with their group. Asking them from a position of power only amplifies the power imbalance, making it harder for students to refuse the request without fear of consequences or at least disappointing the teacher. From their vulnerable position, students may find this stressful and uncomfortable.

No Free Passes

What I learned from this experience was that my professor did not have enough knowledge about Orange Shirt Day or the colonization of Canada to teach about it. This is why they reached out to me, knowing I could do the work for them. When people in positions of authority—such as teachers and administrators—do not know the history, they may use the excuse that they were never taught. As Susan Dion writes, there is no "free pass" when teaching, and no excuse for being ignorant or hurtful.[6]

Dion writes of the "perfect stranger" approach some educators take toward Indigenous history and education.[7] Dion points out that teachers can replicate and continue educating the way they have been educated in the dominant norm of society and may feel fearful of challenging the discourse that has been ingrained as knowledge. This positions educators to become rule followers and protectors of the post-contact historical dialogue. This position protects the teacher and enables them to sit safely within what they comfortably know and don't know. In other words, stating "I didn't know" allows educators not to challenge the narrative and deepen their understandings of our shared colonial history of this place known as Canada today. The TRC report and the MMIWG report reinforce that we are in an urgent moment in time where it is critical for all educators to move away from the "I didn't know" phase and lean into the discomfort of educating themselves about this history so that they do know and can teach it.

Holding Space

"Holding space" may be a newer term used in educational spaces today. For me, it means that there are some moments in time where it is critically important for educators to stop the class and address something that has happened, whether that is a racist or otherwise inappropriate comment, before moving on with the lesson of the day.

In one of my classes as a grad student, I was sitting through a class discussion, facilitated by two non-Indigenous professors,

When having conversations about race, validating feelings and emotions is key to creating a space of comfort and safety.

---

that revolved around what land acknowledgements mean, and what it means to be an immigrant on this land. This allowed for the conversation to revolve around how the white students felt when talking about this topic, which they found challenging. People said many inappropriate comments, but the most hurtful one was when the conversation came to residential schools and a student said, "Well, we need to remember that the people who came here [settlers], came from a society that boarding school was the norm and it was a privilege..."

I was trying my best to be open and just listen, as my Elders have taught me to do. But in this moment, after sitting through more than an hour of harmful conversations and comments, I could not stay silent any longer. I spoke up and gave the class a lesson on the devastations of Indian Residential Schools. I pointed out that they were prisons for our children, not schools. The white student tried to take back their words, but I did not allow the white voices to keep dominating the classroom space and conversation. Educating others was not my role in the class, but neither professor stopped the conversation or appeared to know how to hold space to stop the ignorant, hurtful, and harmful words that needed to be challenged.

After I finished my mini lesson on residential schools, another IBPOC student spoke up and addressed the professors about how the space was creating more trauma for students whose families have suffered so much trauma already. Now, the professors had an opportunity to unpack what had just happened and create space for some healing from the trauma that had occurred. Instead, they gave the class an early dinner break and did not talk about what happened any further. After the dinner break, the professors simply told the class that we needed to talk nicely to one another because some people's feelings were hurt. All this created more harm to those who had experienced the trauma in class.

This played out in a higher education context, but similar scenarios play out at all levels of education. If educators don't know how to hold space, they may—even inadvertently—create unsafe learning environments for IBPOC students. This is not unusual for classrooms spaces for IBPOC students; this is something that they must navigate on a daily basis in the education system. While also navigating how and what they need to learn.

When students do not feel safe in a classroom, they are in a constant state of fear and learning anything becomes extremely difficult. This is why it is so important to stop and hold that space, even if the conversation is uncomfortable. Not addressing the harms perpetuates them, and IBPOC students then leave and get pushed out of education because of how difficult it is to navigate.

Comments Left Unsaid

As educators, we need to be able to understand ourselves not only as educators but also as human beings and racial beings within a racist system and society. Knowing this, we then can address the dynamics of a class that has a mix of IBPOC students and white students. Derald Wing Sue's book *Race Talk and the Conspiracy of Silence* gives educators guidelines to create spaces for difficult conversations within the classroom. Sue states that it is critical for us, as educators, to know our positionality (where we are located in relation to social identity, as in race, class, ethnicity, gender, sexuality, (dis)ability, etc.) and be willing to share this with our students.[8] This helps to create a space of openness, honesty, and trust. As an educator you also need to be aware of your own racial biases and blank spots that could influence you and your teaching.

When having conversations about race, validating feelings and emotions is key to creating a space of comfort and safety. From my experience, I can say the most important thing to do is to address any harmful comments immediately. Leaving them unaddressed causes more trauma to the students who internalize the words. Silencing of voices and ignoring the comments is an action, an action of racism. Inaction is an action. If an educator chooses to do nothing about the harmful words and actions within their classroom, they are perpetuating harm and racism in the educational space.

Not a Place for Me

In the book *The Anti-Racist Writing Workshop* by Felicia Rose Chavez, my favourite quote is, "I thought I hated school, but in fact school hated me."[9] When I read this, so many things fell into place for me. I started to understand why I had so many challenges within the system. I knew from a young age in my schooling that this was not a place where I could be successful and flourish. School taught me the opposite of that—that I was not smart, capable, and human. There was nothing within the curriculum, the walls, the books, or the stories that were about me. School only reflected the white colonial story and what the all-white teachers could connect with. This place was not made for me, an Indigenous person, to succeed, nor any IBPOC students.

Recall, from the welcome chapter, Kirkness and Barnhardt's statement about what Indigenous students need: "an education that **respects** them for who they are, that is **relevant** to their view of the world, that offers **reciprocity** in their relationships with others, and that helps them exercise **responsibility** over their own lives."[10]

If these words were in practice in educational spaces for IBPOC students, the experience would be transformational. This is what my experience was like during my master's degree in Indigenous Education and Leadership. I experienced education through a lens of what was needed for Indigenous students to be successful. The class was composed of all Indigenous students, almost all Indigenous faculty, and all the readings were from Indigenous authors and scholars. I had no idea about so much. I learned so deeply about protocols, Indigenous ways of knowing, Indigenous peoples, and about myself as an Indigenous person. I finally saw myself. I felt what it was like to be seen and heard within education, and it was unreal. I had been traumatized through twenty-plus years of colonial education but finally felt what it must feel like all the time for white colonial society to be the only thing taught in class.

This program created Indigenous warriors, warriors in education, warriors in educational spaces, and warriors in academia. Out of my class, almost all of us hold leadership positions that will help change education. That's amazing! If you think about that for a moment, there were seventeen of us in total—sixteen Indigenous women and one Indigenous man—who were seen and heard, seventeen of us who saw ourselves and gave one another the confidence that we needed to be changemakers. If that could happen for us, imagine what could happen for students if we gave them that at a younger age in the K–12 system. A place to be seen, heard, and honoured. What an amazing transformation could happen for Indigenous people of this land.

Questions for Reflection

- How are you curating your resources to ensure balanced representation and the inclusion of historically silenced voices?
- How are you reading about identities other than your own (and beyond your preferences) to become more informed about the experiences of others?
- What are you going to do to make change happen for IBPOC students in your classroom?
- How has your education shaped who you are as an educator?
- How does your own education impact the students in your classroom?
- If you could change anything about your education, what would it be?
- What are the things you can put in place to better support IBPOC students in your classroom?

Resources

Bonilla-Silva, Eduardo. *Racism without Racists: Color-Blind Racism and the Persistence of Racial Inequality in the United States.* 3rd ed. Lanham, MD: Rowman & Littlefield, 2010.

CBC Radio. *Unreserved.* Podcast. https://www. cbc.ca/radio/unreserved.

Maracle, Lee. *My Conversations with Canadians.* Toronto: Book*hug, 2017.
Sabzalian, Leilani. *Indigenous Children's Survivance in Public Schools.* New York and London: Routledge, Taylor & Francis Group, 2019.
Talaga, Tanya. *Seven Fallen Feathers: Racism, Death, and Hard Truths in a Northern City.* Toronto: Anansi, 2017.
voicEd Radio. *Anti-Racist Educator Reads.* Podcast. https://voiced.ca/project/anti-racist-educator-reads/.

3

Colonialism in the Classroom

Settler colonialism isn't something one just gets over; it's woven into all aspects of our experience, and those strangling threads are too often invisible and all the more wounding as a result.

DANIEL HEATH JUSTICE[1]

PLAYLIST

"Alright," music video, song by Supaman, featuring Neenah

"Indomitable," music video, song by DJ Shub, featuring Northern Cree Singers

"Calling All Dancers," music video, song by DJ Shub

"All Nations Rise," music video, song by Lyla June

Scan this QR code for links to these videos.

FOR THIS CHAPTER I thought it would be important to talk through some of the ways colonial education shows up in classrooms because we have spent so much time in the western colonial education system. As Marie Battiste shares in her book *Decolonizing Education*, we have all been marinated in eurocentrism, which makes it difficult to see something that is so normalized. One of my favourite resources for looking at colonial education systems is called Equitable Math (equitablemath.org). This site, geared toward grades 6 to 8 math students, outlines clearly how colonialism impacts the math classroom and our teaching in classrooms. It also provides a yearlong workbook with steps to change teaching practice.

As I go over some of the ways, please know that these are not the only ways colonialism shows up in education. These are just a few examples. I encourage you to always look for other ways it unfolds in the classroom.

Western Colonial Education

The western colonial education system is set and rigid. A key marker of this: the system is controlled by the clock. The clock dictates when we start and finish, when we work, and how much time we have for learning. There is always a sense of urgency in the classroom because we have to know things by grade 1 to go to grade 2 and so on. If students don't reach these markers at the

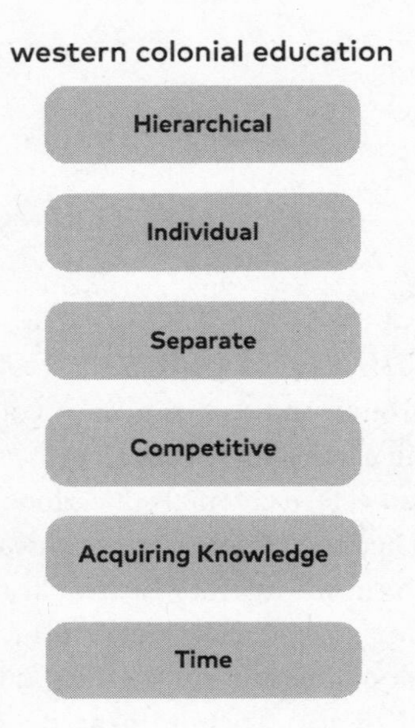

set time, then they fail or fall behind and always seem to be trying to make up for the lack of time to learn in the system. The system is also grounded in the written word and follows those who have come before us who have written the knowledge that we all must learn. This focus on the written word leaves out so many cultures and knowledges that are grounded in oral traditions.

Colonialism also focuses on the individual in the class. It separates the students into groups according to the year they were born but does not account for the individual learning processes. One of the most challenging ways colonialism is embedded into the system is through the concept of there being only one right answer. This one right answer dictates a right-and-wrong mentality in the classroom. It unfolds as always having only one way to show your understanding or only one way of knowledge production, and only one person in the room holds all the knowledge to teach. This "banking concept" of education is something that Paulo Freire speaks about

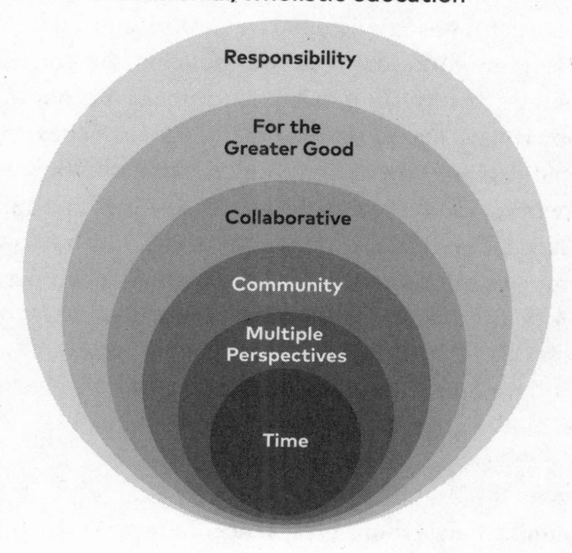

in his book *Pedagogy of the Oppressed*.[2] My understanding of this concept is that the teacher in the classroom holds all the knowledge, and the students are just consumers of this knowledge, passively taking in all that is taught and told to them, without any input or thoughts of their own.

Colonialism is very much an "or" way of thinking, which is in contradiction to Indigenous knowledges that are an "and" concept of thinking. "Or" is thinking about knowledge as "either this or that," end point. There is no other way to look at it and only one right answer. "And" is a concept of "this and that and that" and so on. The more knowledge and worldviews we bring into the knowledge-making process, the better it makes it for all of those creating the knowledge.

As I unpack my own understanding of knowledge systems, I have been working on the two graphics above for a while. As I build upon them, they are helping me see how my understanding of teaching and knowledge systems unfold in the classroom.

The hope of these visuals is to demonstrate the differences between a western colonial framework and a decolonial/wholistic framework, so we can start noticing how colonialism impacts the school system today. The intention is not to separate knowledges, just to share how these knowledges operate so we can explore how to shift our teaching practice. I am a visual person and for me to understand something I like to see it. This is how the diagrams came to be. I also know that this is my perception of the school system through personal experience and study. There may be many other ways to view and show this.

Let's have a look first at the components of the stacked colonial model.

Hierarchical

The colonized classroom experience delineates the roles of student and teacher. As with Freire's "banking concept" of education, the teacher has all the knowledge that they impart upon the students. The students are the empty vessels to be filled with knowledge, which they regurgitate back to the teacher. This hierarchy of authority and individualism leaves little room for authentic relationships to evolve. The classroom has a power imbalance, putting the student and educator in polarizing positions that work against each other, rather than in relationship with each other. Power relations are a constant tension when working in the colonized classroom. In my educational experience, I have been silenced by this authority in the classroom. And at times when I am the person in authority in the classroom, I see that students say what they think I want to hear in order for them to pass a course. This diminishes opportunities for authentic learning experiences. When one person holds power over another, the possibility for an authentic relationship to be built is tainted.

The hierarchical system in education starts at the government level. Provincial governments in Canada develop and approve curriculum, approve and regulate teacher education programs, and regulate teachers and qualifications for the system. They control the levels of education, and the steps for students to work their way through the system. The system is legitimized and audited by the government. This colonial way of education reproduces the social hierarchy of the western colonial mindset and puts power relations at the core of the system.

Individual

Students in the colonized classroom are graded and looked at individually. They are judged solely on their own thinking and understanding of the information that has been handed out to them. This individualism is the goal of colonization. Dwayne Donald[3] and Leanne Betasamosake Simpson[4] speak of this within their work about colonization. They define colonization as a severing: of relationships with each other, with the land, the waterways, the more-than-humans, our communities, and our families. This focus on the individual aspect of students teaches students to look inward only at themselves and does not allow the collaboration of the knowledge-making process. When everyone is only ever working in their own best interest, it does not allow for students to look outside of themselves and at their larger accountability to others.

Separate

In high schools and higher education, we do not allow for subjects and ideas to cross over into other subjects. In high schools all subjects are separated into their own time block, which perpetuates the thinking that all subjects are stand-alone knowledge, dismantling the understanding that we are all connected and separating the knowledge-making process. This divide and conquer approach separates education from relationships and real life as a whole. For me, I see this as the compartmentalizing of knowledge and knowledge-making processes. That there are so many compartments within the education system speaks to how colonialism wants us to be separate from the subjects we teach and learn. As outsiders, we consume knowledge rather than seeing ourselves as part of the whole.

Competitive

The education system has always been a competitive place, built upon rewards and accolades for those who do well within it. If you get good grades, you are acknowledged for your achievements, make the honour role, move on to the next level, and so on. Those with the highest grades are selected first for post-secondary education, and admittance to post-secondary education requires a certain grade point average. This puts the pressure on the students to achieve high grades and this pressure starts at the moment when students realize that grades matter and are the only thing that counts. They start to compare themselves with other students, asking them what they got for marks. To apply even more pressure, all you have to do is add in the bell curve—you are only as smart or not smart in comparison to your classmates. Competition drives who gets scholarships, who is accepted into the "best" universities, and who gets the highest-paying jobs.

I know from watching my children go through school, the conversations about how they are doing in school revolve around "Well, I did better than . . ." The focus is on how much better they can do than others. What they have learned and the process of learning is not part of the conversation.

Acquiring Knowledge

Acquiring knowledge is what the western colonial education system is built on. Through this colonial lens, this acquiring piece is for yourself personally. It is not set up for the greater good of all. The individual gathers the knowledge they need to receive a level that allows them to continue on to the next level. Acquiring this knowledge and receiving the completion documents then allows for them to show their "smartness." This lens develops an understanding that education and knowledge can become commodified and rigid. Consumers of education just take in knowledge and are less engaged in the knowledge-making process.

Time

As I spoke about at the beginning of this section, time is a foundational piece of the colonial education system. The clock guides and rules educational spaces. Every day, the bell sounds and we go to class, the bell goes and we start class, then it marks recess, lunch, and so on. Students are under the continuous pressure of the clock with report cards that set them up for learning on a timeline. The linear concept of time often limits the ability for knowledge, learning, and growth to unfold in the space that is needed for deep understanding. Knowledge is a commodity acquirable only within a set time frame, distributed by the teacher, and received by the learner. This leaves little to no room for those who do not learn and understand within the time frame given; therefore, they "fall behind" or "fail."

Decolonial/Wholistic Education

I want to circle back to the beginning of this book where I talk about decolonization. I know that we will never be at a moment of time that we are in a decolonized education system. I believe that everyone has been impacted by settler colonialism, just impacted differently. When I think about education through a lens of wholeness, this is how I think of decolonized education.

Decolonized education focuses on the whole being rather than the parts, and relationships are the key.

Through my eyes, decolonized education focuses on the whole being rather than the parts, and relationships are the key.

Responsibility

When I personally think about responsibility, I think about how it is my responsibility to nurture and care for the next generation so that they will know what they need to know to survive, as within Indigenous communities when you are a holder of knowledge. A knowledge holder is responsible for the knowledge they hold and to pass it on to the next generation. This is not a process of learning just for oneself; it is for everyone who comes after you.

Looking at education as a responsibility and not as certificates to gain is a different worldview. I work toward creating spaces in the academic context, not because I want or need the accolades that come with this work. It is a responsibility so that Indigenous voices can continue to be in the ivory tower (university) and make space for those who come after me. When I am in community and listening to Elders, they always tell us that the knowledge they share with us is not from them; it is from our ancestors. The Elders are passing it along to us, for us to carry it forward to the next generation. This is not about acquisition or ownership. We are responsible for holding knowledge, and responsible for passing it forward.

For the Greater Good

Thinking about responsibility, it is also connected to the greater good. When I personally think about for the greater good, I believe it has deep roots to the lineage of ancestors that have come before me. During the longhouse celebration for my master's degree, the Elders in the room reminded me and my cohort that what we had learned in the program is for the greater good of the community. Not only am I benefiting from this learning, but the community also benefits from my learning. As a cohort we needed to share our learning, to bring it back to community, and to help others with the knowledge we have gained. Knowing that I am part of a larger community, I needed to take care with my learning, because I have a community to support with this knowledge. Which is in contradiction to acquiring knowledge for yourself, and for the betterment of only you. It is for the betterment for all of those in the community and for the next generations that depend on you.

Collaborative

Collaboration is a critical piece of the knowledge-making process in many Indigenous communities. It has many different names within communities, such as "binding the mind" or "common bowl." How I view this process is influenced by the experience of watching Elders speak with each other about the stories of the long ago. They always speak from what they know about the story and then ask others to share what they know. This practice then builds the story together as a whole, each person having a piece to share. Building the knowledge together is a collaboration.

Academic Nel Noddings's research[5] shows clearly that students who work together and share their learnings with others do better in the learning process. This speaks to the importance of working together in the knowledge-making process.

Community

Relationships and community are at the core of decolonial/wholistic education. Indigenous academic Shawn Wilson talks about relational accountability in his work.[6] My understanding of this is that we have a collective responsibility to each other in the knowledge holding, and the knowledge-making, process. With that, everyone within the community is responsible for everyone else's learning as well as their own; it is a joint effort. In some Indigenous communities, the learning process happens with a group of people, engaging in knowledge-making and learning together, in multi-generational groups. This allows for everyone to be a participant in the learning and teaching together, over a span of multiple lived experiences and perspectives. Each member of the community is responsible for the building of knowledge and passing on of knowledge.

When you are a part of a community of learning, it is not a solo endeavour. It is a collaborative group experience, where many voices and knowledges can come together, to build upon everyone's understandings, allowing space and grace for many voices to shape the knowledge. This process of knowledge-making gives a more diverse perspective of learning and understanding.

Multiple Perspectives

Multiple perspectives are also a foundational piece of decolonial/wholistic education.

Cindy Blackstock[7] and Niigaanwewidam James Sinclair[8] speak of the plurality of ways of knowing, the "and" of building knowledge rather than the "or" perspective of the world.

The connection of this worldview to education is that education should not be a "this or that" but a "this and that and that . . ." This allows for recognizing and honouring many ways to look at the world and at knowledge.

Including multiple perspectives also honours all students within the educational system and their worldviews. The multiple perspectives of the world allow for students to gain a deeper understanding of the world that they live in. These multiple perspectives create understanding of the complexities of how race, racism, and oppression are embedded into society. As I have mentioned, students in the classrooms need not only mirrors to see themselves but also windows to see others. If we give students the opportunities to learn about all different cultures, worldviews, and perspectives within the education systems, students will see the world as whole and not only through one lens.

Time

In many Indigenous communities, time is felt differently. Things take the time they take. As I have watched my children grow in ceremonies in community, they are getting much better at not asking when things will be done. The ceremony will start when it starts and ends when it ends. This is tied into the learning process as well. When you start the learning process, it ends once you have learned the task you are learning. This is different for each person, because we all have different strengths and abilities. Looking at time through a decolonial/wholistic lens reveals that education is a flexible and organic journey of understanding and learning. It also is nurtured and rooted in relationship.

A Community of Learners

For me, decolonizing means looking at what we do in education and educational practice differently. We look at our classrooms and students as a community of learners, working together, learning, growing, and deepening our understandings of the world around us.

This comes with collaboration. As I always tell new educators, education isn't a solo gig. We understand more in groups where we can learn from each other, talk with each other, and build upon each other's understandings of the world. Sitting together and unpacking a topic or a piece of learning, listening to how others view the information, and how they are taking in the information, are critical pieces to learning. There have been so many historically silenced voices in education that creating space for these voices to be shared and heard allows for a deeper understanding of knowledge and the knowledge-making process for everyone.

Colonialism in Classrooms

Because the education system has been built upon the western colonial model of education and, as educators, we have had at least seventeen years in the system, it can be hard for us to see how colonialism affects our classrooms. As a way of creating a critical lens, I'll mention here a few key examples of how colonialism unfolds in the classroom.

Focusing on getting it right. I see this in my own post-secondary classrooms when students come in anxious and worried about not getting their assignment "right." "Please, Professor Roberts, can you just tell me what to write down so that I can get a good mark?" This hits to the core of what needs to change in education. If we are so centred on just getting the right answer, rather than looking at the process of learning as a whole, we miss out on opportunities for students to be creative, to think outside the box, to be excited to step into the learning process, and to want to learn. This is challenging in post-secondary because students have had so much time in the system that they can't always let go of this thinking.

It also occurs in the K–12 system. Students are trained early in the mindset that there is always just one answer to things, one way to look at things, and that over and above everything, the final mark is what counts. With so much emphasis on good grades, students lose sight of the bigger picture of what education could offer. My educational experience in my master's program transformed me as a human. I would like to believe that this could be a typical, daily experience for all students, no matter the age or grade, if we changed the process of education.

Independent work and practice. This is another way that the colonial system has built barriers and compartments for learning. The work we do is usually independent work and practice, graded independently, and collaboration in learning is frowned upon. Not just by educators but by the students as well. We all know when the teacher says "group work," the eye rolls and groans follow, because no one wants to get stuck doing all the work for the whole group. If we could support the collaboration process on a continual basis in education, this perception of group work could change. We could emphasize the value of students learning from those around them. I look at this through the lens of a musician, knowing that I could make music on my own, but when I gather with others and they add their brilliance to whatever I'm playing, the outcome is so much better than I could have done on my own without their support and knowledge of their own instruments and contributions to the process.

Class participation. When I was a child, class participation meant putting up your hand when you knew the answer to a question. The expectation was that you showed that you understood and could participate in the conversation. This kind of set criteria, that participation means verbal or written comments, favours those who already have the confidence to speak up. Not all students may feel that they can take up such space. Especially students who the system was not made for.

Students who have been historically silenced in classrooms tend to use silence as a shield to protect their well-being. Timothy J. San Pedro's research addresses how Indigenous students make a conscious choice to stay silent within a western colonial classroom instead of engaging with knowledge that does not acknowledge their existence.[9] When Indigenous students and their ancestors do not have a voice in the curriculum, they learn that the curriculum is not for them. Tying speaking up to marks for participation is not an equal playing field for all students within the classroom. It benefits students who feel confident and who see themselves within the curriculum and books. This structure doesn't allow for all people to have voice.

Grading students based on what they do not understand. When students are tested on their memorization of information, marks are deducted for all the answers that they do not know or remember in a given moment. This practice enforces memorization and regurgitation of information, creating consumers of knowledge rather than participants in knowledge-making. In my educational experience, this practice does not always allow students to engage or to understand the learning process. It is a method, but I don't see it as a way to honour the process of really understanding the knowledge being shared. Consider all the things you had to memorize for tests. How much of that information do you still know today? I think about the biology courses I took in high school and post-secondary, for example, and memorizing of all the parts of so many organisms. Today I cannot remember any of that information now. The marker of knowledge of what you remembered for a test doesn't always impact how much you know as a human.

Mistakes. When we frown on students' mistakes, we drive home the narrative of always needing to have the one correct answer for every question. This same mentality makes us fearful of changing up our own teaching practice, because the education system has drilled into us that we always have to be right and never make mistakes.

Mistakes are a place where deep learning happens. We learn more from our mistakes than we do from things that are easy and right all the time. In my classrooms, I encourage mistakes as a welcome opportunity to relook at students' work, giving students opportunities in how they can improve upon what they have already learned. If they don't fully understand the first time around, I give them an opportunity to show me again. There is always room for improvement in all the work we do, so how can we improve on it?

In the context of a class assignment, if a student hands in work that was not what the teacher was looking for and the teacher feels they have missed the mark, then a typical practice is to give the student a low mark, let's use an example of 2/15. This mark shows us that the student needs some more time to learn and grow from the assignment. If we allow the space and grace for the student to retry and take the opportunity to build on their existing knowledge, then we are inviting deeper learning to happen. If instead we say, "Well, you missed it on this assignment; do better on the next one," we may be detracting from the student's self-esteem—a defeat by education. If they continue to receive low grades without an opportunity to revisit the work and improve upon their knowledge, then showing up gets harder and harder for them.

By the time students reach post-secondary education, the pressure of getting good grades is intense. They have spent so much time in the education system worrying about grades and marks that some send themselves into a tailspin if they get anything a little wrong. Some students cannot recover from this anxiety and just leave programs. Or they start asking instructors to just tell them what they want students to write so they can get a good mark. This defeats the purpose of the learning altogether.

When we allow students the opportunity to try and take risks, and revisit their work to gain the knowledge they need within the work, then we are creating space and grace for students to be successful—not only in the work but in their feelings about themselves in the class. What I have noticed about students who have the opportunity to relook at their work and to speak with me about their work is they have gone on to do amazing things! The work they do after talking and sharing some other ideas with me is generally so much better than it would have been had I just said, "Well, you missed the mark and you just didn't receive a good grade" and moved on. Their learning expands, their understanding expands, and they really engage in the work.

I do, we do, you do. The colonial education system is structured for students to fall in line with what it wants them to know and be able to do. First, I show you the way to do it, then we do it together, then you do the work on your own. And I mark you on how well you copied me. I followed this model as an educator because I was taught this way, and then that was reinforced in my teacher training. The complication with "I do, we do, you do," is that we are reinforcing the idea that there is only one right way to do the work and we are the authorities that show students how to reproduce it just like the way we do it. This assimilation style of education does not encourage students to come up with ideas and think through problems on their own; it diminishes their creativity and free thinking. If teachers are the only ones who determine the right way to do things, we deprive students of the opportunity to think about how they see the work. We lose opportunities of creativeness and of learning from different worldviews of the work. This hierarchical approach silences students in the classroom and in the learning process.

THIS CHAPTER has covered just a few of the ways that I see how colonized classrooms operate for students and educators within the system I work in. Know that if you start to look critically at the system, you will find more ways. Now, let's explore how to think critically about bias hidden in curriculum.

Questions for Reflection

- In which ways have you seen colonialism play out in classrooms?
- In addition to what was covered in this chapter, are there other ways that the colonial narrative might play out in classrooms?
- Why is it important to do your part in disrupting the colonial narrative in your classroom and/or school?
- In what ways are you disrupting the colonial narratives in your classroom or school?
- In what other ways can you disrupt the colonial narratives?
- How can you support mistakes in the learning process?

Resources

Archibald, Jo-Ann (Q'um Q'um Xiiem). *Indigenous Storywork: Educating the Heart, Mind, Body, and Spirit*. Vancouver: UBC Press, 2008.

Chavez, Felicia Rose. *The Anti-Racist Writing Workshop: How to Decolonize the Creative Classroom*. Chicago: Haymarket Books, 2021.

Cote-Meek, Sheila. *Colonized Classrooms: Racism, Trauma and Resistance in Post-secondary Education*. Halifax, NS: Fernwood Publishing, 2014.

Davidson, Sara Florence, and Robert Davidson. *Potlatch as Pedagogy: Learning through Ceremony*. Winnipeg, MB: Portage & Main Press, 2018.

McCoy, Kate, Eve Tuck, and Marcia McKenzie, eds. *Land Education: Rethinking Pedagogies of Place from Indigenous, Postcolonial, and Decolonizing Perspectives*. London and New York: Routledge, 2017.

Muhammad, Gholdy. *Cultivating Genius: An Equity Framework for Culturally and Historically Responsive Literacy*. New York: Scholastic, 2020.

Simpson, Leanne Betasamosake. *As We Have Always Done: Indigenous Freedom through Radical Resistance*. Minneapolis: University of Minnesota Press, 2017.

Tuck, Eve. *The Henceforward*. Podcast. www.thehenceforward.com

4

Hidden Curriculum

We all know that we can go through life convinced that our view of the world is the only valid one. If we are interested in new perceptions, however, we need to catch a glimpse of the world through other eyes. We need to be aware of our own thoughts, as well as the way life is viewed by other people.

LEONA OKAKOK[1]

PLAYLIST

"Warrior Song," music video, song by Edzi'u

"Indigenous in Plain Sight," TEDx Talk by Gregg Deal

"Indigenous Language Revitalization," TEDx Talk by April Charlo

"Little Star," music video, song by iskwē

"The Unforgotten," live performance for CBC Music's First Play Live, song by iskwē

Scan this QR code for links to these videos.

LET'S START this chapter with an analogy. When a fish is swimming in water, does the fish know that the water is there and supports their life? Or is the water "invisible" to the fish? The same could be asked of a society's cultural norms. Cultural norms are things that people often don't question or even think about. Like when people say, "Hey, guys!" "Guys" is used a lot in daily life and in classrooms. But is everyone in the space a guy? Does everyone identify as a male? If not, then is this the right term to use? You would never say to a mixed group of men, women, and non-binary people, "Hey, gals!" or "Hi, women!" This would sound quite strange to the ear. So then why is the term "guy" acceptable to call a mixed group of people? Could it be that our cultural norms are biased? This is one term to think about; can you think of others we might use?

This example suggests the reason why it can be so hard to change the education system. In schools, we tend to do what we have always done and teach what we have always taught. What is important in Re-Storying Education, in decolonizing your practice, is to question what might be underlying in the things we have always done. Could our practices be racist? Problematic for historically silenced voices? Could ways of teaching be seen as oppression? And most importantly, who benefits and who is at the centre of our teaching?

Let's consider a well-known example taught in schools to see how implicit biases are embedded in the curriculum.

Potentially Damaging "Norms"

I remember looking at Canada's Food Guide as a child and learning about it in gym class and nutrition class. This guide is handed out at doctors' offices when you have babies and the diet it promotes is said to be the "norm" and a proper diet that everyone in Canada should be eating. But is it? What do we know about the food guide? What do we know about the students in the classroom? Let's unpack this a little.

The guide suggests that a healthy meal includes half a plate of fresh fruits and vegetables. What I am curious to know is if all students in my classroom have equal access to these foods. The questions I need to know are:

- Do my students live in a remote community that makes it challenging to access the food recommended by the guide?
- Do the students in my class live in poverty and is the food recommended by the guide affordable for them?
- Do the students make the choices about the food brought into their homes?
- Does the food in the guide represent the cultural foods that the students in my classroom eat?

These are just some things I question about the guide when I think about bringing it into the classroom. As educators, we must look deeper into what the guide is telling us as a society: that there is only one way to look at food.

If we teach the food guide, and start off by explaining that it is a resource upheld by the government and doctors, can we be sure we are not harming students? What if the student goes home believing this and does not see these foods in their home? If the student's family cannot access the food recommended by the guide, how might that affect the student? Physical education teachers in high school usually will ask students to write a food journal to show their eating habits and grade them based on criteria from the guide. Is it fair to grade students on something that is so variable and often not within their control? This practice layers another stressor on students, about how they feel about themselves, their culture, and their family.

If we look more deeply into the food guide and the history of nutrition research in Canada, another unsettling fact is revealed. The architect of the food guide, Lionel Pett, was a major player in a series of experiments conducted on malnourished children in residential schools.[2] A 2013 article by Ian Mosby[3] revealed that in the 1940s and 1950s, Canadian nutritionists, supported by various facets of the Canadian government, studied students in the residential school system. Researchers knew that the children were underfed and often malnourished, and they used students as their experimental groups and control groups. In some cases, the nutritionists used the children to test foods that could not be legally sold in Canada, to see what it did to bodies and whether they could get the food approved. The health of the students in the schools was not an important factor for the research. The research now shows that the long-term effects of constant hunger for survivors of residential schools has led to a whole series of problems for Indigenous people today, such as higher risk of diabetes and higher risk of obesity.[4]

This history hides in plain sight while the food guide is taught in schools all across Canada. It promotes the idea that following its guidelines is needed to live a healthy lifestyle. Having a one-size-fits-all food guide for the mosaic of the Canadian population is unrealistic, and we should be thinking about how we can bring more perspectives and worldviews into the conversations and teachings of this guide.

If I were to teach with the food guide in my classroom, I might:

- Ask students in the classroom to think about the food they eat at home. What would their food guide look like if they created one that reflected their culture and what they ate at home?
- Encourage the students to engage with a critical eye, asking who Canada's Food Guide was written for. Who is represented in the guide and who is not represented?
- Use Canada's Food Guide and the First Nations, Inuit and Métis Food Guide to start some conversations about why these guides might be problematic.[5] Talk about why the First Nations, Inuit and Métis Food Guide cannot be a one-size-fits-all, because of the large, diverse population of Indigenous peoples across this place known as Canada today. Plus, because the food for Indigenous peoples is clearly tied to their location, land, and resources available, how can this one guide support all groups? How could we change this? What would it look like?

Examining Hidden Biases

All educators should be focusing on where the hidden curriculum is in the work they do. I was reading a research study about Fountas & Pinnell, the early literacy intervention books for struggling readers.[6] The study was not looking at whether the books were good for learning to read; the authors, Deani Thomas and Jeanne Dyches, were looking at the stories and the implicit messaging the books were telling the struggling readers.

The study found that the books showed racial bias and discrimination within the stories. Although the numbers break down a little differently for fiction and non-fiction, the overall pattern was that white characters tended to be portrayed

What is the underlying narrative of the stories you use in the classroom?

as "heroic, determined, innovative, and successful." While the non-white characters were portrayed as "inferior, deviant, and helpless."[7] They also found that many of the non-fiction books, considered to be delivering information based on facts, included a majority of white main characters that were scientists or highly educated people. In fiction books, when leading characters were people of colour they were often portrayed as deviant, criminal, and dysfunctional. If the characters were people of colour, they were either Latinx or Black. Asian and Indigenous characters were not represented at all in any of the books.

These kinds of narratives are so embedded in the curriculum that unless we use a critical lens to question "who, what, when, and how" in all the materials we read, we might inadvertently be sending the message to IBPOC students that their stories don't matter, or that they are the problem. What books and stories do you use in your classroom? What is the underlying narrative of those stories?

For example: If you use a book that tells a story about a little Black boy who does not have enough money for shoes, do you talk about how this story contributes to the false narrative that all Black children are poor? Or are you making sure that the next story is about Black excellence and achievement? If we only talk about Black trauma, then that will be the only story for Black people in the classroom. The same is true for stories about Indigenous peoples. If we only tell the stories of Indigenous trauma, then people will never know about all the amazing, brilliant Indigenous stories that are out there in the world.

Likewise, what we *show* students in the classroom matters. If, when you are creating presentations or slide decks and it is always easy to find images of people who look like you, and if you always see images of people who look like you reflected in visual media, then you might not even notice that the same is not true for others. Or if you rarely find any images of people who look like you, you may get tired of searching and start to select any pictures that you find instead of continuing to look for equal representation. I encourage you not to give up and to keep looking.

Making sure that we take the time to select images that students in our class can connect with is so important. Selecting images of people who students might not see on a regular basis is important too. Images should be varied in terms of representation—gender, sexuality, race, (dis)ability, religious affiliation, etc. Representation in educational spaces provides validation and support, especially for equity-deserving populations or those that have been historically underrepresented and silenced within education and society. Having diverse representation can be helpful in reducing negative stereotypes about other groups. If students can see themselves and their experiences reflected in images, they learn about the many possibilities for themselves that exist in the world.

HAVING LOOKED AT some of the history and starting to consider the effects of colonialism in the classroom, as well as learning to identify hidden biases in curriculum, we are ready, in the next chapter, to turn our attention to practices we can take on to actively decolonize the classroom.

Questions for Reflection

- In the books or textbooks you use for your classes, what stories are being told about a wide range of people and cultural backgrounds?
- In fiction: How are the main characters portrayed? Do the portrayals fall into cultural stereotypes? How are you talking about the characters in the story? Are you including many different perspectives of these characters?
- In non-fiction: Are there images of people from a variety of cultural backgrounds? What do the images say about the people represented?
- Who are the authors of the books and other resources you use in your classroom? Whose voice is dominant in the readings? Whose voice is dominant in your classroom? Whose voices might be missing?
- Who are the students in your classroom? How are you bringing in voices that represent your students, and that students can connect with racially and culturally?
- In what ways can you incorporate more voices within what you are teaching? How might students take what you are teaching and reflect it back to you through their culture? (For inspiration, see my example of using the food guide as a launching point for students to create their own guide to reflect their culture in the "Potentially Damaging 'Norms'" section.)
- In what ways does your teaching support students to debunk stereotypes?

Resources

Battell Lowman, Emma, and Adam J. Barker. *Settler: Identity and Colonialism in 21st Century Canada*. Halifax, NS: Fernwood Publishing, 2015.

Manuel, Arthur, and Grand Chief Ronald M. Derrickson. *Unsettling Canada: A National Wake-Up Call*. Toronto: Between the Lines, 2015.

McGee, Meghan. "'As a Matter of Policy, Kids Were Hungry in Residential Schools': The Dark History of Canada's Food Guide." Healthy Debate, April 18, 2022. https://healthydebate.ca/2022/04/topic/history-canadas-food-guide/.

Mosby, Ian, and Tracey Galloway. "'Hunger Was Never Absent': How Residential School Diets Shaped Current Patterns of Diabetes among Indigenous Peoples in Canada." *Canadian Medical Association Journal* 189, no. 32 (August 14, 2017): E1043–E1045. https://doi.org/10.1503/cmaj.170448.

Richards, Sydney. "Canada's Food Guide: The Hidden History of Canada's Nutrition Recommendations." Canadian Feed the Children, March 2, 2023. https://canadianfeedthechildren.ca/the-feed/food-guide-2023/.

Tennant, Zoe. "The Dark History of Canada's Food Guide: How Experiments on Indigenous Children Shaped Nutrition Policy." CBC Radio. *Unreserved*. April 19, 2021. https://www.cbc.ca/radio/unreserved/how-food-in-canada-is-tied-to-land-language-community-and-colonization-1.5989764/the-dark-history-of-canada-s-food-guide-how-experiments-on-indigenous-children-shaped-nutrition-policy-1.5989785.

5

Re-Storying Educational Practice

The task of educators is to love children enough so as to invite them to engage in the world's renewal, not as we imagine it, but as they will, in their coming into our presence.

HANNAH ARENDT[1]

PLAYLIST

"Nature's Song for the Time Being," song by Fontine

"Red Winter," music video, song by Drezus

"I Believe," music video, song by Cree Nation Artists, Chisasibi Community

"Stay Connected," music video, song by Supaman

Scan this QR code for links to these videos.

I HAVE SPENT the last few years travelling around the province of British Columbia and the Northwest Territories supporting school districts, educators, administrators, and Indigenous education departments with learning about decolonizing their practices. One of the questions people ask me most frequently is, What does decolonized practice look like within the classroom? This is why I thought it was important to dedicate this chapter to sharing with you some of my personal teaching practices that are decolonizing, to show you some concrete ways of entering into the work of Re-Storying Education.

At the core of my educational practice are the four "guiding questions" of Daniel Heath Justice's book *Why Indigenous Literatures Matter*:

1. *How do we learn to be human?* What are the experiences, customs, traditions, and ceremonies that define our humanity? How do we realize the full potential of our physical and imaginative human embodiment with healthy bodies, hearts, and minds?

2. *How do we behave as good relatives?* What are our relational rights and responsibilities to one another and to the other-than-human world? How do our literatures help us realize these relations in meaningful ways?

3. *How do we become good ancestors?* How do we create the kind of world and relationships that will nurture those who

come after, and give them cause to thank us rather than curse or grieve our destructive selfishness? And what does literature do to help guide this work?

4. *How do we learn to live together?* What are the social and intellectual structures, conventions, and considerations that reduce or manage conflicts and encourage harmonious relations across our varied categories of difference? How do our stories offer helpful models for those efforts?[2]

These questions ground my teaching practice in why I do this work. I am an educator because I want to make sure that the next generations of Indigenous students see themselves as educators and have the opportunity for a better education, one that includes their voices. I believe this will happen if the system shifts how we educate the next generations and ground the work with relationships. Justice's questions support such a shift by placing relationships at the core of the work. He begins by asking, "How do we learn to be human?" This, for me, is at the core of education: seeing each other as human beings and honouring each person in a human way. This means that we treat each other as kin, as a relation. As Justice states: "kinship makes peoples of us through responsibilities to one another."[3]

This leads right into the next question, "How do we behave as good relatives?" I see my role in the classroom as an Aunty, which means that I love you like crazy and I will still hold you accountable and expect the very best from you.

"How do we become good ancestors?" Being good ancestors is foundational in most Indigenous communities, because of the belief that what we do today affects the next seven generations to come.

"How do we learn to live together?" This question speaks to me in this moment as we navigate a new sense of the world around us that was negatively impacted by COVID-19. Having to isolate and change how we do things affected how we interact with each other. So, relearning how to be kind and gracious with each other is critical.

All of these questions guide my approach to the practices I offer you in this chapter. The first I'd like to talk about is Circle Work.

Circle Work

There are many practices I do in classrooms that focus on decolonized teacher practice, and one of the most important practices is Circle Work. I have used this practice in the K–12 system, when I was an administrator with my teaching/staff teams, as well as in post-secondary classrooms. Circle Work is a way to set up community, connections, and relationships within the classroom. The Circle Work tool that I share with you in this chapter can be used by any educator, Indigenous or non-Indigenous, and is not a ceremonial tool or spiritual practice. The pedagogical framework that I have put together for Circle Work consists of five concepts:

- Relationality
- Decolonization
- Witnessing
- Anti-racism
- Time

Relationality is a foundational concept within Circle Work as the practice is built upon the understanding that everything we do in education is based on relationships: with students, with educators, with communities, and with families. Building strong relationships helps educators do the work of teaching, because if students feel like their teacher cares for them and wants them to succeed, then students are more willing to participate and be engaged in their classroom.

Circle Work is a practice of **decolonization** in the way the physical space encourages engagement with the knowledge-making process. Positioning the educator as a facilitator and a participant, in the learning community, this removes the hierarchy of power and domination found in western colonial classrooms. It also encourages all participants, including historically silenced voices in the classroom, to share their voice as knowledge holders of their own lived experience.

Listening in Circle Work is more than just a passive process. It is what is known as **witnessing** in some Indigenous communities. Witnessing is a way to engage with oral traditions of sharing Indigenous knowledges. If you are asked to be a witness, you are being asked to fully participate and be present in the moment. This participatory practice is more than just listening to someone share their knowledge with you. It is asking you to listen deeply, listening to listen, not listening to respond, so that you can take in what another person is sharing and understand their words. Witnessing is critical in Circle Work, as it is asking the participants to fully show up, listen with an open heart and mind, and be present with one another in the circle.

For all the reasons we've covered in previous chapters and more, **anti-racism** and anti-racist education is critical in the work of education today. We must create educational spaces where IBPOC students are welcomed in, shown that their voice matters, and assured that they have a place within the classroom. Circle Work allows the historically silenced students the opportunity to share their worldview. It also allows students who *have not* been impacted by racism and other forms of oppression an opportunity to hear how others who *have* been affected by racism and oppression live with it on a daily basis.

When teaching, **time** is a commodity. Educators are always negotiating what they need to do by when. So, when I suggest doing Circle Work, they get nervous because it takes up time in the classroom. Circle Work is an invitation to creating a different concept of time in the classroom, acknowledging that we cannot always rush from one thing to another, that we can create space for deep connections to learn from one another. This work values the time it takes to sit together as humans, to be able to fully see each other.

While the educational benefits of using Circle Work in the classroom are many, some of the key benefits are building:

- Community within a classroom
- Opportunities for students and educators to connect and create relationships
- Communication skills with one another
- A foundation for learning about how to be anti-racist with each other

The practice of Circle Work has been transformative for my students and me within my many classrooms. In my own teaching experiences, I have seen that when I gather students in a circle, the energy in the room always shifts. Circles allow for the students to feel the connection to each other and the synergy from this collective energy. This connection centres and grounds the relationships we have with each other; it gives us a deeper understanding of what it means to care for each other. With everyone in the circle facing one another, with no one in front or behind, there is a space of honouring and the colonial hierarchy of control and power is removed.

Circle Work does take time, but I have seen it build strong, lasting friendships and relationships that have endured beyond the classroom. This foundation of communication skills and relationships is so beneficial when you move into doing other work within the classroom. Building a community that knows each other and feels comfortable with talking to each other allows space for the students to flourish.

Practice: Setting Up Circle Work

The ways I use Circle Work are different for different times. Circles can be used for multiple things within the context of your classroom. I sometimes use Circle Work as a soft, gentle start to the day; sometimes it's a light check-in with some fun questions to ask. But other times, when people need to connect and there is lots going on, I let the group know we'll do Circle Work as a temperature check to see how everyone is doing. At the end of class times, I may use Circle Work as a verbal exit slip, or a place to process learning, or as a connection before we leave.

For whatever purpose we are doing the work, here are the steps I take to set up Circle Work in a classroom.

Clear the space. I begin by preparing the room. I move any tables and large objects to the outside of the circle. I place chairs in a circle formation, or I clear space for everyone to sit on the floor or to stand in a circle, whatever works best in a given class. I usually set it up with the number of chairs needed for the amount of people who are in the class, which helps me to know when everyone is there.

Put devices away. I ask participants to put their technology away, so there are no distractions, unless people need it for accessibility. When we are not distracted by devices and the outside world, we can focus on what is happening in the room around us, being fully present in the work. As educators, the importance of hearing the voices of those around us is a key piece in learning about how to shift our lens to a decolonial and anti-racist view.

Acknowledge everyone. If this is the first time you are doing Circle Work with your class, I suggest opening in a good way. I see this as preparing and acknowledging each other. When I open the circle as the facilitator, I start by acknowledging who I am and where I have come from, in a similar way to how I opened this book. I let the circle know who my ancestors are and where they are from. Then I ask the students in the circle to share their name and who their ancestors are, if they know and wish to share.

If you have done circle with this group before, you can open the circle with questions, check-ins, or whatever feels important for that day.

Give participants choice. When opening the circle, it is respectful to remind people that they always have a choice to speak or not to speak. They are encouraged to share but also know it is okay not to share. Creating the space for people to be open with each other, to share their human experiences through their story, is how we create a community of care. Know that this community of care happens when this work is consistent. Getting to know each other and listening to each other takes time, so this needs to be a practice. It will be up to you as an educator to decide when you do Circle Work; for me I do this at the beginning of every class in post-secondary and in K–12. As an administrator, I did it for every staff meeting. Practising circles at the start of each day, or each class, or each week, or each time you do work together creates a decolonized space and a strong community. It will be up to you as an educator to decide when it fits best for you and your class.

Remind people to witness. Reminding everyone of the importance of being a witness within the circle is critical—every time you do Circle Work. When it is time for someone to speak, everyone else is asked to be a respectful witness to their words, to listen with an open heart and mind. No one else should be talking at the same time. Everyone's contribution to the circle is of equal value. If people forget this, I will look in their direction with my Aunty eyes or quietly ask them to stop talking and to listen.

*Circle Work is
an invitation to
creating a different
concept of time
in the classroom.*

Ask people to stay. That all voices are honoured and heard within the circle is so important. And so, once a circle is opened, everyone who is in the circle stays until the circle is complete.

Close with sharing. At the end of the circle, I always allow for people to share whatever they are feeling or whatever they would like to put into the circle before we close it for the day. This gives people the opportunity to close the circle in a way that feels best for them.

Jigsaws

The activity of doing jigsaws allows students the space to learn about a topic together, to share their ideas and their worldviews. This tool can be used from grades 4 to higher education. This activity will look different at each level. The younger students will need more supports to do this work. But it is possible to set them up for success. With this practice, students lead their own learning and are active participants. As such, it removes the typical hierarchy in the classroom, where the teacher is the knowledge holder and students are merely receptacles of information.

I use jigsaws often and find them most useful when I need to teach about really heavy topics, such as residential schools. A jigsaw supports me as an Indigenous faculty member teaching non-Indigenous students about topics they might not know a lot about and who might find the information challenging. Because the jigsaw does not position me as the sole knowledge holder in the room, I can be out of harm's way if a student pushes back against the knowledge being shared. The jigsaw allows for students to look at the information together and unpack what they have learned before we move into a larger group discussion about the impacts of the topic.

Jigsaw activities have many layers of learning and teaching built into them. The first layer is that you invite students to be active participants in the work by researching and educating one another about the given topic. Researching could mean reading a book aloud together in sections, googling information, or looking to other non-fiction resources (podcasts, news reports, documentaries). This practice shows students that they are a part of the learning process. It teaches students how to look for information they would need to know to teach it to someone else. In the teacher education classroom, this sets up new teachers in a good way to acknowledge that they have a part in the learning process as researchers of the knowledge they need to teach others.

Once students have researched their topic and shared it with the group, the group processes what they have just learned together. They talk about what they already knew and didn't know, and about any discomfort they may be feeling. This discomfort may not go away, especially with difficult topics, but it provides students the opportunity to learn to sit with the discomfort within smaller groups, which allows them to feel more comfortable in asking and discussing questions with each other, before going back to the larger group.

When students are doing this work, I walk around the room and listen in. I allow opportunities for group members to connect with me if they need me to be a part of the discussion in their group. Once the small groups have talked and shared, I bring everyone back together in a circle to talk through what they learned in the process. I also ask them what they might still be wondering about or if they want to share what their conversations were like. Now not everyone in the group will share, so you can either have exit slips for the day, a reflection journal for the work, or maybe even a project that gets created out of the work they did together. This will support you in seeing what the students have learned.

Practice: Jigsaw for Indigenous Education Reports in Canada

As we covered in chapter 1, many reports over the last one-hundred-plus years talk about Indigenous education, Indigenous peoples, and the relationship with the Canadian government. This jigsaw activity helps students understand what has been done—and not done—with the many reports. It is an exploration of the progression of the work in Indigenous education and the relationship with the Canadian government. This jigsaw is suitable for students in grade 4 to higher education. What follows are the steps that you can follow when doing any jigsaw practice in the classroom.

Organize groups. I start by dividing the class into small groups. For example, if your class has thirty-five students, you would create seven groups of five people per group.

Share material and questions for the work. Each group can select one report, making sure that each report is covered. They are then tasked with researching about the report, answering the questions provided in the "Questions" section to follow, to learn more about it. For younger grades, you can have preselected places for students to use for their research; for older grades you can give them more freedom. The questions will guide the work.

Reorganize the groups. Once the groups have learned about their report, I reorganize the groups so that one person from each report is in a group together. So, in a class of thirty-five people, with seven groups to begin with, you would now have five groups with seven members each. Each member of these new groups shares what they learned about their report, allowing for the group members to teach each other about all the reports.

Time the work. Depending on time and the material that students are reviewing, I generally give the first groups of five people twenty to thirty minutes for researching/reading/connecting with the topic. The second groups consisting of seven people each would have sixty to seventy-five minutes to share about the reports.

A smaller number of people per group may need less time.

Scale to grade levels. The substance of the content and the time allotted for each portion of the practice also depends on the grade level of the students. For younger grades, you may want to provide them with prepared resources and allow for more time. You could also divide this work up, allocating some time in class to research/read/connect with their topic and, in a subsequent class, having them come together in groups to discuss. You know your class best, so make your best judgment call.

Use variations. You can vary the practice based on your class:

- If you have a smaller class and don't have time to cover all the reports in one lesson, plan to do them over two classes, with half the reports one day and half the next day.
- If you wanted to create a group project for each report, the original groups could work together and share their project with the class. For example, you could plan a gallery walk with the reports.
- For younger classes, you can select only a few questions from the lists below for the group to answer. Or they might need more guidance about how to look for information if they are just learning how to do research.

Assess. Here are some suggestions for assessing your students on their learning:

- You can assign specific questions for an exit slip for the day.
- You can ask them for a journal reflection about their report, or all the reports.
- You can ask for an overview of all the reports. This could be written, in video form or other visual art form, or whatever way works best for the student.
- You could do Circle Work, to give everyone an opportunity to contribute an oral reflection.
- You could use a T-Chart, to fill in under the headings: "before we did this work, I knew..." and "after we finished this work, I now know..."
- You could also have students create a pie chart that includes all the key points from each report.

Questions

What follows is a list of the reports I use and suggested questions to go with each report. These are only suggestions. You are welcome to add more questions or create your own questions to tailor this to work best for your class.

Report on the Indian Schools of Manitoba and the Northwest Territories by Dr. Peter Bryce

When was this report written?

Who was Dr. Peter Bryce?

What was his role in the government?

What did his report find?

What were the recommendations?

What happened to Bryce after the report was written?

Hawthorn Report (*A Survey of the Contemporary Indians of Canada: Economic, Political, Educational Needs and Policies*)

When did this report come out?

What was happening during this time that prompted this report to be written?

What were the findings of this report? What was the new catch-phrase used for what they wanted Indigenous peoples to be from this report?

What were the report's recommendations for education?

What did the government do after this report was completed?

How have things changed because of this report for Indigenous peoples?

Indian Control of Indian Education

When was this policy paper published?

What did the government do that forced the coming together of the National Indian Brotherhood?

Who wrote this report? Why was it so important?

What was the report asking for within Indigenous education?

What reforms was the report asking for in education, both on and off reserve and in public schools? Have any of these reforms been accomplished to date?

Royal Commission on Aboriginal Peoples (RCAP) Report

What event was a precursor that led the government to establish the Royal Commission on Aboriginal Peoples (RCAP)? What caused the event to happen?

How long did the event last, and how did it get resolved?

Why did the government think it was necessary to establish the RCAP?

When did the RCAP release its five-volume report?

What were the major findings for education from this report?

What is the legacy of the report? How many calls to action were there in this report? How many have been accomplished?

How does this report help with legal cases about Indigenous issues today?

United Nations Declaration on the Rights of Indigenous Peoples (UNDRIP)

When was this report published? How long did it take to write?

What rights does UNDRIP affirm for Indigenous peoples?

When the UN General Assembly voted on UNDRIP, what countries did not vote to support it?

What provinces in Canada have signed on to uphold UNDRIP? How has it been implemented or not implemented in Canada?

How have things changed for Indigenous peoples since the UN General Assembly adopted UNDRIP?

Truth and Reconciliation Commission (TRC) Report

When was this report published?

What happened in the Canadian courts as a precursor to this work? Who contributed the payment for the TRC report to be written?

How many calls to action are there in this report? How many are focused on education? What are they?

How many calls to action have been completed to date?

How has this report changed education in K–12 and higher education across Canada, if at all?

Missing and Murdered Indigenous Women and Girls (MMIWG) Report

Note: I would only use this report for older students. I would suggest grade 10 and up with lots of prep and front-loading with trigger warnings. You will need to prepare students for potential triggers and know that sexual violence will be a topic within the report. Prepare students for how to have respectful conversations about these topics.

When was this report published?

What was happening in the Canadian courts that prompted this work?

How many calls to action are there? How many calls to action focus on education? What are they?

How many calls to action have been completed?

How has this report improved the lives of Indigenous women and girls today?

What was this report focused on changing? How does it address systemic racism?

Conversation Starters

The above are just some of the many reports about Indigenous education in this place known as Canada today that students can look at. Some great conversation starters after the review of these reports could be:

- How do these reports create change in the system?
- Is doing mass-scale reports creating change in the system?
- Why do you think governments and school districts call for reports to be written?
- Do you believe that there could be another way to effect change in the system other than using reports?

- What are some ways you could think of that could make change possible?

These questions are just that: questions to engage in a dialogue about how the government uses reports, spends time and money on reports, and then many of the reports get put on a shelf to be forgotten about with no action to follow up on the calls to action. I would love to talk about other ways that we could engage in critical change work, as a society, outside of using reports.

Resources for Further Research

Here are some places for further learning. There are more than these, but these offer you a few places for entry points. I link to all of these resources on my website, carolynroberts.net. Scan the QR code at the back of the book to access them there. You can also do a simple online search of these terms to find some useful resources:

- Adolescent UNDRIP (the UN Declaration on the Rights of Indigenous Peoples written for thirteen- to eighteen-year-olds)
- Beyond 94 (an interactive CBC website about where Canada is at with the TRC calls to action)
- Indigenous Watchdog Calls to Action (a useful resource on where Canada is at with the TRC calls to action)
- First Nations Child & Family Caring Society (a national networking organization to support caring for Indigenous children)
- Dr. Peter Bryce, *A National Crime* (a 1922 book about residential schools in Manitoba and Northern Ontario)

- "Kanesatake Resistance (Oka Crisis)," *Canadian Encyclopedia* (an online resource that describes the 1990 event)
- *Kanehsatake: 270 Years of Resistance* (an NFB film about the Oka Crisis by Alanis Obomsawin)
- *Beans* (a film about the Oka Crisis by Tracey Deer)
- White Paper of 1969 (more information about this can be found on the Indigenous Foundations website)
- "Red Paper: A Counter-Punch to the White Paper" (a blog post from Indigenous Corporate Training Inc.)
- National Indian Brotherhood/Assembly of First Nations: Our Story (about how the Assembly of First Nations came to be)
- Hawthorn Report (*A Survey of the Contemporary Indians of Canada: Economic, Political, Educational Needs and Policies*)
- *Indian Control of Indian Education* (by the National Indian Brotherhood)
- Truth and Reconciliation Commission (TRC) report (the Canadian government and the National Centre for Truth and Reconciliation provide resources)
- MMIWG final report (the final report of the National Inquiry into Missing and Murdered Indigenous Women and Girls)
- *Highway of Tears* (book by Jessica McDiarmid about a Northern highway where Indigenous women and girls have gone missing for years)
- *100 Years of Loss: The Residential School System in Canada* (a teacher's guide produced by the Legacy of Hope Foundation)

Book Clubs

Most of the students who have spoken with me about their experiences in the university say that they are in isolation within the classrooms they are in. Many students tell me that in their other classes they spend their time listening to the professor talk and rarely engage in conversations with other students. Not talking to other students makes building connections and community with each other impossible. One of my Indigenous-focused courses is taken mostly by students who are in their last semester at university. When I ask for feedback on the course, I hear from students that this is their first class where they actually know other students in the class and actually talk to them inside and outside the classroom. On the one hand it makes me happy that they have made connections. On the other hand it makes me sad that they have spent at least four years in a place without making any meaningful connections at all.

One of the ways in which I help to support connections in my class is through book club work. Now I have used book clubs in my class for a while, but when I started working with Sara Davidson, she helped me reshape my book clubs in a way that supported the work better. Thank you, Sara, for your expertise and teachings.

The books I use in book clubs are always a reflection of what we are learning in the class together. Sometimes I have all students read one specific book, but I prefer to have many different options of books for students to read so that they have different entry points into the work. Students form small book clubs around the same book, and the book club follows a structure.

In many of my courses, the key point of book club is to learn and grow from reading Indigenous authors, building connections with students and setting up students in a good way to have critical conversations about the book they are reading. This practice also assures that the students can discuss the work we are doing together with others in the class. This community building is key. If a student is away from class, I can connect with their book club members to see if the student is okay, and they can share the learning of the day with the absent student.

A book club is a great tool for connecting a group of students who might not have otherwise connected. It allows space for smaller conversations about the learnings. There are many skills developed in book clubs, such as researching, connecting knowledge from other resources, facilitating discussions, writing questions, and taking notes, and they also set up students for success working in groups. I find that, when working in groups, students hold one another accountable because they have to educate and share their learning with each other.

Practice: Book Clubs

Book clubs are a great tool for students. I will give some examples of how that can look for younger and older grades. What follows are some suggestions of ways to engage in book clubs. Keep in mind that you know your students best, so when setting up book clubs with students, select the tools that will best support your students.

Creating groups. When I set up book clubs, I usually gather groups of four to five students, maximum. I keep them small so that people have a place to share their voice. With larger numbers, voices can be lost in the mix. In my university classes I usually allow my students to make their own groups. In younger grades you might want to create the groups yourself.

Offer readings. Book clubs meet once a week to talk about their readings of the week; this could look different in your classroom, it could be twice a week, or every other week; this is completely dependent on your schedule. The reading relates with the learning we are doing in the classroom. Note: I also take the time to read through the book myself so that, when I connect with the students, I know what they have read and can facilitate larger group discussions about the reading.

Laying the groundwork. The preparation of book club is just as important as book club itself. It is important to set up guidelines for how the group will operate and how to have productive conversations that will support learning. When you introduce book club, talk to students about how to discuss the work in a way that will support learning as well as being respectful to all members of the group. Know that in book club group discussions, all voices within the group must be included. This is an opportunity to share ideas and understandings of the work the class is doing together. Encourage book club members to speak up and share. This may take time and practice for some, so make a point of talk time in the group. I usually ask one member of the group to be the guide for the work that day. This role shifts each time, so that all book club members have an opportunity to lead the group. The guide needs to be mindful of who has spoken and who has not and to ask all members if they would like to share that day.

Also point out that there will never be one right answer in the work that you do. There will be multiple perspectives and with that comes messiness and possible discomfort on some topics. Discomfort is part of how we grow and learn, so I encourage students to sit within discomfort to see what it is teaching them. There is a difference between being uncomfortable and being harmed. Knowing the difference requires awareness in ourselves and in others. Learning to listen to other voices, building capacity for conversations, and building on skills that include how to have difficult conversations are really important in this work. With that being said, I always tell the students that if something is happening in book club that doesn't feel right or is harmful, I need to know so that I can support and address it.

Sharing responsibility. I set up book club groups in ways that will generate responsibility and contributions from everyone in the group. I do this by offering roles to each member of the group. These roles change every week, so that each person's contribution to the work changes. All students must read the material in advance and not just focus on their role, because the expectation is to have discussions about what they are learning from the book.

Some suggestions of roles for book club groups could be:

- **Discussion guide/facilitator.** This person guides the conversation and usually has a few questions prepared for the group to support the conversation about the book. They are also the timekeeper.
- **Connector/researcher.** This person looks beyond the assigned reading for other sources/stories/news that connect with the reading. They share that research with the group and why it connects.
- **Highlighter/focuser.** This person identifies key points that they feel are most important within the reading to share with the group to have a larger dialogue about them. They also bring in some guiding questions for the group about the chapter.
- **Summarizer.** This person will capture the group's discussion so that members and the teacher have a sense about what is being learned from the book. This can be in point form or paragraphs.

These are just a few ideas for different kinds of roles within a book club. There are many ways to make this grade appropriate; I encourage you to do some research on lit circles for more ideas.

Give prompts. Some younger grades may need writing prompts for this work. Some older grades may also benefit from support with discussion questions. Here are some suggestions of prompts for book club conversations:

- When I read this passage, I felt like the author was addressing...
- I did not know about ______________ and this chapter helped me understand...
- I am making ______________ connections with what is being said...
- When the author was talking about ______________, it made me wonder...
- I appreciated...
- I was surprised by...

Depending on your class and groups, you will know best how to support them in this work. You might write some questions for each chapter, or you might allow students to find their own voice and way through the work. I like to support some of the more challenging conversations with prompts so that students who might not want to talk about a certain topic may use my questions instead of having to come up with their own. I will do this to support when I know groups are struggling. This, of course, would look different for each group and each grade.

Assess. This practice involves small group work and you cannot physically be in all the groups at the same time, as you will be walking around the room having small moments of listening in to the discussions. You can, however, be responsive to what the students are saying about the book and how in-depth their understanding is of the book with their conversations and questions. Here are some other ways to gauge students' understanding:

- Ask them to hand in summary/reflections about their work together.
- Do exit slips for each student.
- Invite students to create something that shows their learning from reading the book. This could be a presentation, an art project, a written project, or whatever their creative mind can think of.
- Have students create a T-Chart that shows what they knew before they read the book on one side and what they have learned on the other side. This reflects their growth.

Younger Grades

I think that book clubs are a great activity for younger students too. Preparing and setting them up for success in the work will take some time, but they are capable of it. Younger students need guiding questions to follow, a clear format for the book club, and clear expectations for each role within the group.

For younger grades, teachers might:

- Select a student to be the group guide of the day to keep the group on track.
- Give the guide two to three selected questions that the teacher has prepared about the book they are reading to talk about with the group.
- Invite the students to add in their own questions if they would like.
- Provide a space for the group to write down their thinking after the conversations together, so that you as the teacher can see their learning.

This is a way to start the work with younger grades and, as they get older, teachers can give them more space to create their own questions and make other connections. This will all be dependent upon the students, how they are engaging in the work, and how successful it is within your classroom.

Teaching about Cultural Appropriation

Educators need to be able to find authentic voices for the classroom. This helps to interrupt the single-sided story that has been the main story of education in this place known as Canada today. Indigenous voices have been silenced in Canada and the Canadian education system for over 150 years. That educators and students hear stories about Indigenous peoples, from Indigenous peoples, is critically important. This way we all learn about the amazing and brilliant people who have been living with and on this land for over twenty thousand years from them—not told through the eyes of someone else.

For me, the term "cultural appropriation" describes when someone, typically from a dominant culture, takes elements or customs from a marginalized group or historically silenced group and uses it out of context or inappropriately adopts it, without the knowledge, understanding, or respect for the culture it was taken from. Then not acknowledging how these actions affect the marginalized group.

"Cultural appropriation" is a relatively new term that academics began to use in the 1980s to talk about the problems found with colonialism. Currently we hear this term regularly, as people on social media have been calling out inappropriate uses of cultural artifacts and cultural regalia. One of the longest such conversations is about how sports teams and school mascots use cultural faces, regalia, and items from Indigenous cultures for representation of their teams. So many studies have talked about the harm of this on Indigenous students[4] that I find it shocking that we still need to have these conversations. Another form of cultural appropriation happens when someone, for example, wears an "Indian Princess" costume for Halloween, and this includes dressing up in Hawaiian grass skirts. When these conversations come up, I usually share *Teen Vogue*'s video "My Culture Is NOT a Costume" (available on YouTube), which describes the harm of dressing up as another person's culture.[5]

Another form of cultural appropriation is when anyone who is not Black wears cornrows. Black people have lost their jobs, have been judged, and/or have been denied a job because of their traditional cornrows, while non-Black people wear them as a fashion statement and are praised for it. Cultural appropriation also includes non-Indigenous people wearing what looks like a traditional Indigenous headdress or making traditional headdresses out of paper in a classroom for all students to wear. These are examples of what cultural appropriation looks like.

I give these examples in the conversations I have within my classroom about cultural appropriation, but what I like to focus on are books and authors. This is also a critical conversation to have about art and artists. Cultural appropriation within books and art is also complicated and can look like someone creating a book, story, or art piece based on a culture other than their own and selling it for profit. Now this is a really broad statement, and it is not a simple answer to work through. These conversations are complicated and have many layers.

What we as educators do need to be mindful of is that looking out for cultural appropriation is a practice; it is an ever-shifting conversation that is not static. A question I always get asked when talking about cultural appropriation in books is, "Can you please give us a list of books that are okay to use within the class?" My answer to that is, "Yes, I can give you a list, but know

As Jesse Wente writes in his book Unreconciled, *"Cultural appropriation is Canada's tactic, a colonizer's tool. Indigenous people didn't invent it; we just suffer its consequences—so why should we have to endlessly explain it?"*

---

that the list would be okay for just this moment, and it could and most likely will change over time."

I know that this seems like a frustrating process. Teachers usually give me a look like, "Are you kidding me?" This work is complicated and always growing and changing. We must always be willing to check our resources because as we learn more, some books that were okay yesterday may not be okay today.

This important conversation must be had with all students in the classroom as well. I encourage the conversations as soon as students start to look at art, books, and music. They need to know the difference between appreciation and appropriation. I will share with you how I approach this in my classroom as it is something everyone can do.

Also, speaking about cultural appropriation and representation addresses the inclusion of authentic voices in the classroom. Part of the work in decolonizing, and Re-Storying, is making sure that classrooms are not just telling one story, one narrative, and one way to view the world, like Chimamanda Ngozi Adichie reminds us, the danger of a single-sided story.[6]

To change this narrative, we need to be intentional about including stories and curriculum from IBPOC authors and educators. From my own personal experience in education, I did not start to read stories and articles from IBPOC writers until my master's degree. This is after seventeen years of only learning about the world through a western colonial, white lens. This is not unusual for IBPOC students. We have spent so much time looking at the world this way, it is time to be intentional about bringing in more voices. My hope with connecting multiple voices/worldviews to the work of decolonizing and Re-Storying is to show how we can shift education to be more inclusive for all students within the classroom.

Understanding Cultural Appropriation

Usually when I start the conversation about cultural appropriation, I ask the following series of questions for the students to answer. This is a starting point to the larger conversation about cultural appropriation.

What is cultural appropriation? Cultural appropriation is an extraction of cultural significance. When someone usually from the dominant culture takes pieces, elements, or cultural traditions from a culture they do not belong to, these items then become distorted or lose all meaning and this becomes detrimental and disrespectful to the culture it was taken from.

Why does cultural appropriation matter? A single-sided story of Indigenous peoples in Canada has been historically told by non-Indigenous people. This has not been the real story of Indigenous people because it has always been told through someone else's worldview. This means that what people know about Indigenous peoples is not actually the real story. Keep in mind that those with the power to tell the story have no real knowledge or lived experience to tell the true story of Indigenous peoples. From the history of this place known as Canada we can see that the Indigenous peoples' stories and voices have been silenced. It matters that Indigenous people tell their own story, in their own way, so that other people can see and learn about Indigenous peoples from Indigenous peoples, who have the lived experience and authentic knowledge. As Jesse Wente notes, "Swapping the truth of Indigenous life for a colonizer's invented interpretation creates the gap in understanding that has so long framed First Nations, Métis, and Inuit peoples as primitive and inferior. That depiction of us and our communities has in turn been used as justification for policies and practices that treated us as something less than full human beings. The harm done is immeasurable."[7]

Who does cultural appropriation hurt? As we can see from the history of the stories being told about Indigenous peoples, we have learned very little about the true story of Indigenous peoples of this land. So, it hurts Indigenous peoples and all of those who have been historically silenced through appropriation. Also, if you are using a book in your classroom written by a non-Indigenous author about Indigenous peoples, you are letting the space in the classroom be taken up by a non-Indigenous person who does not have the lived experience or knowledge that is needed to tell the story in an authentic way. The non-Indigenous person is taking up the space that was supposed to be for Indigenous voices, so it is again silencing Indigenous voices and not allowing them space or voice in your classroom. It also hurts all students in the classroom because it does not allow for them to actually learn about Indigenous people and we will continue in the same spot we are today, with the single-sided narrative.

What can we do to make sure voices that have been historically silenced have space in our classrooms? As educators we can always be reflecting on the curriculum and resources we bring into our classrooms. We make sure we have representation in our classroom in books and curriculum from historically silenced voices. We also make sure we check from time to time with the authors and what is being said about the books and curriculum with people who might know more about this, like the librarian, or the Indigenous education department.

Why is cultural appropriation not a simple conversation? It is not simple because the answer is never going to be one way or the other. It will be complicated and shift from time to time. We need to do our best to use authentic resources and listen to the voices of those whose culture is being discussed, as they will know more than us, to guide us in the work. But all educators are responsible for doing this work too.

Vetting Source Material

How can you figure out if a book is okay to use in the classroom? *Google is your friend!* If you find a book on Indigenous subject matter that you want to use, google the author. Answer the following questions:

- Who is the author?
- Are they Indigenous? What Nation are they from?
- Does the resource contain Indigenous stories? Are they the author's story to tell?
- If the author is non-Indigenous, was it written in collaboration with an Indigenous community or person? Not vetted—in collaboration. Words matter.

Knowing the answers to these questions is a first step in the process. Just because a resource checks all the boxes doesn't guarantee it is a good resource. It means that it looks like it could be from an Indigenous person with the story belonging to them, but it might not be the best resource for your classroom. You must review it, analyze it, and make your own decision from there.

As Indigenous people, we always tell you who we are and who we are connected to. We will tell you the Nation, community, or treaty we belong to; it is a part of who we are as people. Please make sure that this information is consistent with the author over a few different websites. If the author doesn't include this information, then most likely it is a non-Indigenous author. In such a case, it is pretty safe to say that if the book is about Indigenous people and culture and the author is non-Indigenous, then I would not recommend this book for the classroom. Know that this is just a first step in the process when learning about how to select authentic books. You must take the time to read through the resource and make that decision if it is a good fit for your classroom.

Another example is finding a book by a non-Indigenous author that was written in collaboration with Indigenous people or communities. Then the conversation turns to whether the author worked with the community to write the book or not. My response is *words matter*. How the book came to be matters. Did the author work with and alongside the community to write what the community wanted to share, in *collaboration* with community? If so, I would see this as a book that has the community voice in it, because it was a collaborative process. If the book was *vetted* by community, this means that the book was written first and then given to community. This, for me, is not okay because the book was written by a non-Indigenous person, from their viewpoint of what they think the community is. The vetting comes after the fact. I would not use this book in my class.

As Jesse Wente writes in his book *Unreconciled*, "Cultural appropriation is Canada's tactic, a colonizer's tool. Indigenous people didn't invent it; we just suffer its consequences—so why should we have to endlessly explain it?"[8] I highly recommend everybody read Wente's book, and the chapter on the power to tell our stories. It is a powerful read.

The questions "Does this book/resource contain Indigenous stories? Are these stories their stories to tell?" are important. For me, these questions are important to ask because we know that Indigenous people are not pan-Indigenous. We do not all come from the same ideas, cultures, and traditions. I personally would not be able to write a book about Anishinaabe culture because I am not Anishinaabe. I am St'at'imc and Stó:lō. Anishinaabe stories would not be mine to tell. When we are vetting resources for our classrooms, we need to make sure that the story and the author are connected.

We are in a moment in time where there is an abundance of amazing Indigenous authors, writing amazing books; please take the time to find and read their stories.

Practice: Teaching about Cultural Appropriation

Having learned about cultural appropriation ourselves, we can extend this learning to our students.

To teach about cultural appropriation, I often do the following. This can be done with grade 4 and above.

Explore cultural appropriation. I have students start off the work by talking in small groups about what they think cultural appropriation is.

I have students ask and answer some of the same questions from above:

- What is cultural appropriation?
- Why does it matter?
- Who does it hurt?
- What can we do to make sure voices that have been historically silenced have space in our classrooms?
- Why is it not a simple conversation?

Share. After the conversations I have students share their thoughts about the topic.

Investigate. We then move into being cultural appropriation detectives, with a "Seek and Find" exercise. In small groups, they find a bookselling website that has an Indigenous selection. Then we take a deep look at the materials being offered. The students choose three different books and consider how they are presented on the website. I ask students:

- Does the book information say anything like "Indigenous" or "Indigenous content"? What words are used to describe the book and what do those words mean?
- Who is the author? Where are they from?

I ground the work in relationships and relationship-building as a core foundation of the work I do as an educator.

- Does the book contain traditional Indigenous stories? Who or what community do they belong to?

This allows for students to practise what to look for in books and resources. I usually ask the groups to research and then present the materials they considered and what they learned about them to the larger class.

Use variations. A variation of this can be looking for headlines about cultural appropriation stories in the news. This connects to real-time issues about cultural appropriation. It also allows the conversation to be more than just about voices within books; it talks about the problem across many different platforms like fashion, movies, TV shows, and with celebrities.

Another variation is having groups research the arguments for and against Indigenous mascots for sports teams and schools. Have the students look up both sides of the argument and then hold a large group discussion about what they learned and how the mascots harm Indigenous students.

One of my favourite videos to share about cultural appropriation is "7 Myths about Cultural Appropriation DEBUNKED!" from MTV and available on YouTube.[9]

THE KEY with this work is that students research and discover many different forms of cultural appropriation and why it is harmful. Having these conversations at younger ages will support people knowing and understanding how harmful cultural appropriation is to people who have been historically silenced.

What's My Role in Making Bannock?

Recently I was presenting at a professional development day about culturally responsive pedagogy and the educators were asking some brilliant questions about how they could authentically step into the work of Indigenous education. They thoughtfully did not want to overburden Indigenous educators or presenters in their schools. One question was: If, as a non-Indigenous educator, they had taken the time to learn to make bannock from an Indigenous person or Elder, would it be okay to teach making bannock to their class on their own, without having to always ask someone to come in?

First of all, this was a great way to show their understanding that it cannot always be Indigenous people who do this work, that they also need to step up and do the work of teaching too. I appreciated that insight. And my answer may be a little more complicated than a simple yes or no.

What I always encourage people to do—as a first step—is to think and research about the subject, in this case bannock. Why do Indigenous communities have bannock? Did they have bannock before settlement? If not, then what if any kind of bread was used? What happened in Canadian history that made bannock a food source for Indigenous people? (Being forced off our land, being subjected to laws against hunting and fishing, being dependent on food rations from the government, etc.) Teaching about how and why bannock has become a food that is known as Indigenous food in Canada is so important. I want to encourage educators to teach the history and the why of bannock. You can then connect this with other communities all over the world, with what kind of fry bread they have and why. I suggest you have a listen to this podcast about bannock: CBC's *Telling Our Twisted Histories* has a great show about decolonizing words, and the episode on bannock is so insightful.[10] I highly recommend all episodes.

I ended the conversation with the educators by saying that we as Indigenous people should be teaching the cultural pieces of who we are in classrooms. The role and focus of non-Indigenous educators should be teaching about the impacts and harm of colonialism on Indigenous peoples, so that the next generation knows the whole history of this place known as Canada today. So, skip the making-bannock part of the lesson and teach about why we have bannock in the first place. This is where we should start.

Making Connections

As you have read through this chapter, I am hoping that you can see some ways that, through my practice, I have created my classroom to include student voices within the conversations and knowledge-making process. I have also grounded the work in relationships and relationship-building as a core foundation of the work I do as an educator. As a parent, I always know which educators fire up my children, which ones light them up and build their curiosity. I know which teachers take the time to connect and build relationships with my children. I am always so deeply grateful to those educators. Sadly, I also know about the teachers who don't do this. I hear stories of things that harm my children that I also encountered as an Indigenous student. Relationships are always at the core. Students know if you like them or not, if you know their name or not, and if you really care about them as human beings. This is what makes the relationship and relationship-building the most important part of education for me. This includes our relationship with the land, which we'll consider next.

Questions for Reflection

- How do you take the time to authentically welcome students in a humble and respectful way into your building or classroom?
- Where in your schedule do you allow time to build relationships with students and the people you work with?
- How might you incorporate some of these decolonial practices into your teaching practice?
- What steps are you taking to bring in authentic voices into your classroom and vet resources?
- Have you used resources that you later discovered are not okay to use? How did you change your practice based on that learning?

Resources

Brown, Martha A., and Sherri Di Lallo. "Talking Circles: A Culturally Responsive Evaluation Practice." *American Journal of Evaluation* 41, no. 3 (September 2020): 367–83. https://doi.org/10.1177/1098214019899164.

Dion, Susan D. *Braided Learning: Illuminating Indigenous Presence through Art and Story*. Vancouver, BC: Purich Books, 2022.

Graveline, Fyre Jean. *Circle Works: Transforming Eurocentric Consciousness*. Halifax, NS: Fernwood Publishing, 1998.

Justice, Daniel Heath. *Why Indigenous Literatures Matter*. Waterloo, ON: Wilfrid Laurier University Press, 2018.

Maracle, Lee. *Memory Serves: Oratories*. Edited by Smaro Kamboureli. Edmonton, AB: NeWest Press, 2015.

6

Learning about the Land

Remember that we are to walk softly on our sacred Mother, the Earth, for we walk on the faces of the unborn, those who have yet to rise and take up the challenges of existence. We must consider the effects our actions will have on their ability to live a good life.

KANATIIO (ALLEN GABRIEL),
"A Thanksgiving Address," *Looking Forward, Looking Back: The Final Report of the Royal Commission on Aboriginal Peoples*[1]

PLAYLIST

"Water Is Life," music video, song by Lyla June, featuring Oliver Enjady

"Stadium Pow Wow," music video, song by The Halluci Nation, featuring Black Bear

"Let Em Go," music video, song by Supaman

"Stand Up/Stand N Rock #NoDAPL," music video, song by various artists

Scan this QR code for links to these videos.

AS YOU STEP INTO Re-Storying Education, knowing the stories of the place where you live is so important. This chapter describes a way to start to think about the stories you know about the land where you live. I encourage you to engage with your students in the Re-Storying of this land. Re-Storying would mean that you include the story before this story of today of this land. Include the story of the Indigenous peoples of this land, how the land was used before settlement and colonization.

Story is a big part of who we are as people; we tell our stories from our worldview and our worldview is shaped by where we live and the stories that have come before us. Part of my practice as an educator in teacher education is connecting students to the land that they live upon. I want to encourage them to build a relationship with the land and get to know the land as a relation. I invite students to go to places that they are most familiar with and go regularly.

I then ask them to go with a more critical eye. I want them to focus on learning about the story of their location being told today, which includes taking pictures of signs that tell the story of the place. After they have done this, I ask them to do a deep dive online, in books, in archives, etc. to find out what the story before this story was, the story prior to contact with europeans: Who lived upon this land prior to contact? Whose land/territory is it? How did the Nation(s) use this land? How has it changed over time? Is the story of the Indigenous people of this land being told today at this location? If so, how is it being told? The hope of this work is for students to walk away more curious about the land they live on and the story before this story of the land as they know it today. This sets up teacher education students to have more information about the land around them, which they can pass on to their students when they get into their own classrooms. The ripple effect.

Another entry point of this work is to engage with the trees, flowers, fauna, and berries of the territory. I send students out to their favourite spots or other locations nearby and have them look at and find out about the trees and plants that are there. I ask variations of these questions:

- Are the trees, flowers, fauna, and berries indigenous to the area?
- If they are not indigenous, then when/how did they get here?
- How were the trees, flowers, and fauna used by Indigenous communities of the territories?
- Do the plants have an Indigenous name in the language of the territory/land?

Some amazing resources for this information are available: card decks, books, and apps. This practice invites students to be more aware of their environment and connections to the natural environment. This work also starts to help us understand what the indigenous plants are in our area and what invasive plant species are harmful to our area. Knowing what is invasive, knowing what kind of trees are around, helps us as humans connect to the places where we live.

Knowing the territories and history of the land also supports people with their land acknowledgements. Land acknowledgements became more common after the Truth and Reconciliation

Commission (TRC) report came out in 2015, to acknowledge and honour the Indigenous peoples' inherent right to the land that Canada is built upon.

Land Acknowledgements

In current-day land acknowledgements, people often use the term "unceded land." When I first heard this term, I did not know what it meant, so I became curious about it and looked it up. Unceded land means land that has never been bought, sold, or traded. For me, the term "unceded" obscures meaning during land acknowledgements. I believe that words hold great power and if we were to say, "Land that has never been bought, sold, or traded," this would give more power and directedness to land acknowledgements and underscore why it is so important to recognize whose land we are on. This is critical here in BC, where I live, as we do not have all Nations in a treaty relationship with the province. This land was *never bought, sold, or traded.* (It's important to note that even when Nations do enter treaty, that doesn't necessarily mean the land is ceded: "In many cases, the intent of the agreements was the sharing of territory, not the relinquishing of rights."[2])

Land acknowledgements that we usually hear at the beginning of meetings, events, and classes were inspired by the TRC's ninety-four calls to action. The calls to action have instigated many things, including calling upon the Canadian government and Canadians to start engaging in meaningful dialogue about the true shared colonial history of this place known as Canada today. This dialogue contributes to the betterment not only of the Indigenous people of this land but of all people of this land. Land acknowledgements themselves are a necessary first step toward honouring the original caretakers of this territory. The hope of these acknowledgements is for the people saying them and listening to them to recognize, respect, and honour Indigenous peoples and their inherent kinship to the land as original caretakers. This is critical information to share since that history has not been taught in the colonial education system. I see the acknowledgement as a moment to educate those around you, and as an act of decolonization as you challenge the traditional story about how the country of Canada was formed.

From my teachings, Indigenous communities have ancestral protocols that are enacted when welcoming people into their territories. Each community and Nation has their own protocols and ways of doing this work because each Nation has their own unique peoplehood. This is completely different from what we have heard and know about land acknowledgements.

Doing a land acknowledgement is an invitation to all people to share with us their knowledge and understandings of the colonial history of this place known as Canada today, also sharing with us what this history means to settlers on unsurrendered, stolen territory. The hope is that we all learn a little bit more about this history in order for us all to do better in changing the single-sided, colonial narrative that has been perpetuated by the colonial education system. It is an invitation for everyone to deepen their understandings of the colonial history of this land and to hear about the work that is being done to decolonize within all the places you live and work.

When you create your land acknowledgement, please make sure you take the time to know the Nations and territories you are on; most importantly, practise how to say the territories in the language of that territory. There are lots of resources out there for this work and it is possible for the work to change. A few resources to start with are:

- "A Guide to Indigenous Land Acknowledgment," by the Native Governance Center[3]

- "Land Acknowledgments: Uncovering an Oral History of Tkaronto," a video with Sara Roque and Selena Mills[4]
- "Beyond Territorial Acknowledgments," a blog post on the *âpihtawikosisân* website[5]
- "I Regret It," an interview with Hayden King on CBC's *Unreserved*[6]

These are just a starting place. Please make sure to do your own research about how to do this work in a good way in the places where you are.

Here are some of the questions I like to give people when they are creating their own land acknowledgement. Let's think about:

- Who has been displaced in order for us to be here today? This includes the humans and more-than-humans.
- How has colonization impacted the land you live upon? And the peoples whose land it is?
- How does this impact the work you do as an educator/human?
- How does this inform you as an educator/human?
- Knowing this land was never bought, sold, or traded, what is our responsibility to the land and the people of the land?

I was so lucky to have done a land acknowledgement recently as I welcomed an amazing Indigenous author, Waubgeshig Rice, on his recent book tour. I share my land acknowledgement with you so you can see how I made connections to the land and the people of the land. I shared some history and an invitation to expand people's knowledge about the place where we were that evening.

It is such an honour to be here this evening to open this space for the conversations tonight.

The words I spoke in my ancestral language of the Squamish people were, "Good evening, my heart is happy to see you, and my hands are raised to all of you as a welcome to the territories of the xʷməθkʷəy̓əm (Musqueam), Sḵwx̱wú7mesh (Squamish), and səlilwətaɬ (Tsleil-Waututh) Peoples." They have lived with and on this land since time out of mind.

Before settlers came, my ancestors had many village sites all along these waterways that surround us this evening. These lands that we are on today were at one time ideal for fishing, hunting, and harvesting food and medicinal plants. In the long ago, our Elders would say that once the tide is out the table is set, because we had everything we needed to flourish and sustain our way of life for twenty thousand years upon this land and waterways.

These territories were once the places for our longhouses, where we would gather together to celebrate who we were as humans. One of our last longhouses was at the village site of X̱wáy̓x̱way, what is colonially known today as lumbermen's arch in stanley park.

The longhouse that stood there was over two hundred feet in length and was the house of our late Squamish Chief S7ápeleḵ, Joe Capilano. The last Potlatch that was held there was in the mid-1880s, just before the Potlatch ban that was in place for seventy years that made it illegal for us to practise our culture and traditions in this place known as Canada today. There were over two thousand people that came from all over these lands from California to Alaska. In our culture, you were so rich if you had family, and for what you could give away. Everyone leaving a Potlatch always left with a full tummy and gifted items.

As we move into a new way of relationship with settlers today, we the Squamish people are revitalizing our language,

> our community, and reclaiming our lands that were stolen from us with the new building in our ancestral village site of Seṅáḵw.
>
> As an educator, it is my responsibility to give back to the peoples of this land in reciprocity for being here; my action for this is to educate those around me about the history of this land and how colonization has drastically devastated the land and the people of this land. As we listen here this evening, I would like to invite you to think about how you will give back in reciprocity to the peoples of this land.

This is just an example. It is to show you a way you could step into the work. I encourage you to learn about the land where you are and make your own land acknowledgement. Another way to step into the work of land acknowledgements and understandings of how long Indigenous people have been living with and on this land is the beautiful lesson plan called the Bead Timeline. This is a hands-on activity that shows, in a visual form, how long Indigenous peoples have been living on this land and how recently settlers arrived here. This lesson plan can be found on the Comox Valley's Indigenous Education website of School District 71.[7] Métis educator Suzanne Camp teaches us how to create a beaded timeline, starting from ten thousand years ago up until present day. This visual representation is a beautiful way to acknowledge and see how long Indigenous peoples have been here. I highly recommend using this lesson plan and activity in your classrooms for all age groups.

Connecting with the Land

I always like to connect with the work that I ask my students to do, for my own learning and growing. On a road trip in the summer of 2022, I personally did the land assignment that I spoke about earlier in this chapter. Once COVID travel restrictions had let up, my family and I decided to take the trip we had planned for the summer of 2020. My three teenagers, my husband, and I did a three-week drive in our RV up to the Yukon and back to Vancouver. This was a moment of so much writing, learning, and so many connections for me. I used some of our stops as opportunities to learn about the land we were travelling through. I learned so much! I share these stories to show you some of the connections I have made to decolonized teaching practice.

Hell's Gate

The first stop on our family road trip was Hell's Gate; it is a tourist attraction that can be found in the canyon area of lower British Columbia. A tram takes you down to the Fraser River. On the tram ride down, we were told a harrowing story of Simon Fraser and his team riding their birchbark canoe over the rapids. Fraser's thoughts of the river were they were the gates of hell. As said in his journal, "We had to pass where no human being should venture."[8] That is how he named this spot Hell's Gate.

The stories of Fraser are that he was the saviour of this place and should be held in great honour, with so much that points to his greatness. This is exemplified by the river being named after him, and two universities named after him, and the whole lower mainland of BC is named the Fraser Valley. Side note: This is what is known as an "environmental microaggression," where place names and buildings are named after white colonial settlers to the territory. This affects the people who have been harmed by these people in history. Another example is the town of Powell River being named after the Indian agent of the Tla'amin Nation. How might this impact the Indigenous people of this area?

When you exit the tram, there is a massive painted picture of Fraser in his canoe. He is the prominent figure, with one Indigenous man in the background and a few other helpers. This points to the significance of Fraser and his greatness.

When you walk around this area you will see some little shops, a food place, and lookout points that allow you to feel the massive power of the rolling river. While walking along the decks, I noticed some "totem poles"—and I put that in quotes because I was not sure they were authentic totem poles made by Indigenous carvers and they made me feel uneasy. One of the totem poles was a life-size, carved Indigenous male with a colourful feather headdress. I had never before seen a full-sized human like this as an Indigenous cultural piece. I was curious, because Indigenous communities that have feathered headdresses are usually communities from the prairies, which do not have totem poles as a part of their culture. The Northwest Coast communities in British Columbia with totem poles as part of their cultural history have large trees that surround them. The prairies don't have rainforests and large trees; therefore, totem poles were most likely not part of their traditions.

Another pole beside this one was also unsettling. I am not sure that an Indigenous person carved it, because there was no information about either pole at the site. There was no information plate, nothing about the names of the carvers or communities where they were from. After we left, I tried some internet searching and looked at the Hell's Gate website, and I could not find out any information about the poles. Knowing that totem poles are part of the traditions of Northwest Coastal communities, and Hell's Gate is farther inland, I wondered why there would be totem poles here at all.

The story of Simon Fraser at this location is that he was the great white man who found this place, where no one else dare go. But is that true? Driving along the highway, you can see the large number of Indigenous Nations and communities that are present that live in these areas and have lived here for twenty thousand years. But Fraser was honoured for "discovering" the area. How can you discover a place where thousands of people already lived? A Government of Canada website[9] tells us that Indigenous people lived there, and that Fraser would not have been able to travel on the river without the support of the Indigenous people of the area. This leads back to my question: How could anyone say that Fraser "discovered" a place, when there were communities of people living all along the river?

As quoted on the Government of Canada backgrounder page: "As the expedition passed through First Nations' territories, Fraser often sent First Nation representatives ahead of the party to inform the local communities of their imminent arrival and to assure them that the group's intentions were friendly. The Indigenous groups provided the travellers with important information, advice, guides, food, and canoes. Oral accounts of Fraser's travels have survived in many of these communities."[10]

Justine Jawanda shares her findings from Simon Fraser's journals. Fraser says that the Indigenous people here were not smart and he looked down upon them.[11] Images of Fraser's journey were posted all around the Hell's Gate tourist attraction, and Fraser was always depicted at the front while one Indigenous person sits at the back of the canoe. I found this baffling because, during my research, I learned that he did this trip only *twice*. Two times he had travelled on a river that had already been in use for over twenty thousand years and the river was named after him.

In reflecting on my own education, we never questioned the stories being told of white settlers discovering this place known as Canada today. Why were we taught that Indigenous people helped the white settler explorers discover this place but never that this land could not be discovered because Indigenous

Unceded land means land that has never been bought, sold, or traded.

---

people lived here and had been living here for thousands of years? It is Indigenous land. Canada is built on Indigenous land. As the government website states: "Like many explorers and fur traders of this era, Fraser was aware that he needed the assistance and knowledge of the Indigenous Peoples."[12]

Back to the tour. At Hell's Gate, I saw one sign that talked about the Indigenous people and the term used was "Indian." The sign was created in 1963 and had not been replaced. This term is no longer okay to use for the Indigenous people of this land, but no one has updated the sign.

On our way back up on the tram, as a good student, I asked the worker, "Who were the Indigenous people that helped Fraser and what was their story of the voyage?" The answer was, "Well, I don't know that information, but I could ask someone at the front desk and see if they know." For me, this was an education fail. At the very least, workers at a tourist attraction should know the territories of the Indigenous peoples whose land they are working on. Hell's Gate is near Spuzzum, where the Yale First Nation of the Nlaka'pamux people is located. Boston Bar First Nation is north of Hell's Gate, and they are a member of the Nlaka'pamux Nation Tribal Council.

Connecting back to education, if students in our education system were taught about the Indigenous people of this land, then that young worker would be more likely to know and to be able to speak about the true story of this place. They would be able to answer a question about who the Indigenous people were, without having to go ask the people at the front desk. This is part of the work that needs to be done all across this place now known as Canada.

WHAT STICKS OUT for me the most in this story is my own reflection on my own education. Knowing that I, as a student in K–12, never thought about or questioned the stories told in my classrooms as a child, I, now as an educator, need to be intentional with how I talk about the history of this place known as Canada today. I need to allow space for multiple stories within my classrooms, multiple perspectives, and encourage students to have questions and to be curious. This intentional work will then make sure that the next generation is learning the whole story of this land and how it came to be what it is today.

Practice: Understanding Place

As a way to bring in another side of history, you can relate this to any place where you live or visit. Look at the names of places and the bodies of water around you and ask:

- What is this location or body of water named after?
- If it is a person, what was their role in history?
- Why is their name used for this location?
- Who are the Indigenous peoples of this land, and where are they located now?
- What are the Indigenous peoples' stories of this land or body of water?

When visiting tourist attractions and provincial parks, ask:

- Whose stories are they telling in the parks and at the tourist attractions?
- Does the attraction or park provide information about the Indigenous peoples' territory they are on?
- What does it say about the Nations and their history of this location?

- Research the area and find out whose territory it is and what the land was used for prior to contact.
- If the location has nothing about the Indigenous people of the land, how can you hold these places accountable for making sure Indigenous voices are heard?

I think a great project would be to have students research about the area around a tourist attraction and learn about the land and people prior to contact, and to create a story, or story board, or a presentation of how the people of the land could be represented at the place. This would be in consultation with Indigenous communities of the area. Then they could share that with the attraction and see if they would be interested in changing the story they are telling at their location about the Indigenous people of that land.

Barkerville

Our next stop on the journey through BC was the historic town of Barkerville. I have to say my hopes were not high that I would enjoy this location. I was anticipating that the settler's stories would be dominant yet again. I am so happy to report that I was mistaken and that there were Indigenous stories of this place told by Sunrise When the Salmon Come.[13] She is a Secwépemc woman that tells the story of her Great Grandmother Lucy Charlie. She was also so informative about the people of this land. What I enjoyed the most about her was her optimism about all the stories that are told in this location. The stories were from Indigenous, settlers, Chinese, and Black people. She said that to understand how we got to today we have to hear all of the stories of this place. All the good and bad parts of our history make up the story of all of us. Can I just say that I love this so much! In what follows is what I and my children took away from her teachings. After our visit we gathered together and wrote down what we collectively remembered from the stories told to us.

Barkerville is located and has history with many different Nations from the territories surrounding it. Shared on the Barkerville website it says several Nations have history and territory in the area, including Lhtako Dene, Nazko, Lhoosk'uz, Ulkatcho, ʔEsdilagh, Xatśūll, Simpcw, and Lheidli T'enneh.[14] The Dakelh and Secwépemc people used this land for summer hunting and gathering of food and medicines. When winter came, they would move to their winter village, located down in the valley at a place colonially known today as Bowron Lake. We were told that when settlers made Barkerville a permanent settlement, the Indigenous people did not understand why they would want to stay year-round in this location because of the harsh winter weather conditions. That advice did not stop the settlers from moving in; they wanted to gather as much gold as they could find. This is what is known in my Indigenous community as "hungry eyes": The settlers, with their hungry eyes, could only see what they could extract and profit from this place. I think if I were to define colonization of this land, it would be the extraction and consumption of natural resources from this land.

Many Indigenous worldviews are that the land is an extension of the people themselves and is a relation, or kin. I have been taught by knowledge keepers that when we go to the land and harvest cedar bark and medicines, we are to never take more than what we need. Taking care of the land is our responsibility, so that in return the land will take care of us. During the gold rush period, Indigenous communities did not understand why settlers put so much value in gold. Gold was not a valuable rock for the Indigenous people. It was heavy to carry, and it was too soft to make tools with. The only gold that Indigenous communities of the area used was gold flakes, for medicinal purposes, when mixed with other medicines. It helped with arthritis.

Sunrise When the Salmon Come told us that the gold rush settlers would not have been able to survive this place if it hadn't been for the Indigenous peoples' help and support with their knowledge of the land and how to survive. Which makes me wonder why the settlers wanted to decimate the communities with smallpox disease. It is said in communities that the settlers would give smallpox-infected blankets to the Indigenous communities to wipe out the people of the land. In Barkerville before contact, two thousand Indigenous people were living in the area, and after the smallpox epidemic, there were only two people left. It is and always has been about the land. As stated earlier in this book, everything Indigenous people have had to endure and still endure to this day is tied back to the dispossession of their land.

The Dakelh and the Secwépemc peoples have been living with and on this land for thousands and thousands of years. Sunrise When the Salmon Come showed us some of the artifacts that were found in the area that tell the story of this place before settlers. The site where the artifacts were found is now at the bottom of Bowron Lake, because of a massive earthquake in the 1960s in Alaska that shifted the land here. We saw two arrowheads made out of basalt rock, a material that was worth more than gold to the Indigenous people. It was lightweight, so easy to carry, and you could carve it into arrowheads to use for hunting. The rock was also traded up and down the coast in exchange for ooligan grease (fish grease used for so much in Indigenous communities).[15] One of the arrowheads was five thousand years old and the other was eight thousand years old. Holding these items and knowing that our ancestors before us left behind stories for us to carry forward was a huge honour for me. These artifacts confirm that Indigenous people have been living here since time out of mind. Sunrise When the Salmon Come told us that the smaller arrowhead, from five thousand years ago, told us that people hunted smaller animals during this time. The larger arrowhead, from eight thousand years ago, told us that the animals during that time period were much bigger, so the arrowheads needed to be larger to kill them.

The rocks of gold and basalt remind us of the differing worldviews of the Indigenous people and settlers—settlers with hungry eyes could only see what they could extract and sell for profit with the gold from the land, whereas Indigenous people used the rocks as tools so that they could feed their families and communities. They didn't collect rocks; they didn't hoard rocks; they used rocks to feed their families and traded it to other families so they could eat as well. This is what I see as the core difference between their worldviews: Indigenous people using the rocks for survival and settlers using rocks for display, collection, and proof of wealth.

Indigenous worldviews are always about the care of the land and the generations to come. In the summer season in the area around Barkerville, Indigenous communities would build shelters out of willow tree branches that were still on the trees. They would find a circle of willow trees, then gather and weave their branches together to create a rainproof roof for their summer shelters. They would hunt and gather berries and medicines for the winter season. Once they were done for the season, they would unweave the branches and leave the place like they had found it. There would be no trace left behind of people living on the land. This was purposeful. It was left that way intentionally and is what is known as culturally cared for land. The Indigenous people of this area did not cut down the trees unless it was necessary. They did not disturb the land. They borrowed from it and returned it as they found it, which is a completely different perspective than that of the settlers. To create Barkerville, settlers cut down the trees, ploughed the land, and made shelters and houses that took away from the land without giving anything back in return. You can still see remnants of settlers all over this area in Barkerville: cans, tools, and machinery just left in the woods, discarded.

Through the Indigenous worldview of treating the land, trees, and the more-than-humans as relations, or kin, we intentionally treat them with a great amount of care. This is also part of Indigenous worldviews of leaving this place in a good way for the next seven generations. If we use all the resources that we find and decimate the land, then there will be nothing left for the coming generations because it will all have been used selfishly, at one time. There are so many lessons we can learn from this Barkerville stop.

Practice: Worldviews and Land

Through this story of Barkerville I see how differing worldviews shape people and the world around them. Sharing stories about differing worldviews would be a great way to introduce students to other ways of interacting with the world around them.

Some questions that we can ask:

- How can these worldviews help shape your own worldview and understanding of place?
- When hearing differing worldviews, how will you engage with understanding other perspectives?
- What are some ways that people live around the world in different locations? How is that guided by the land they live on?
- When visiting places that share the story of forts and settlements, find out about the relationship the Indigenous people had with the first settlers, and their relationship to the land.
- What kind of dwellings were built by the Indigenous people of the land and how did that support the land?
- How did settlers build dwellings? And how did they differ from the Indigenous people's of the territory?

Alaska Highway

The Alaska Highway is said to be the greatest road ever built. But is it really? Whose story is that? Whose voices do we hear when that story is told? Whose voices are left out of that story? And at what cost? When we think about colonization and how it has affected the land and the people of the land, we also must acknowledge that colonization is so much easier when you have roads.

Our trip brought us to Whitehorse in the Yukon. I felt so thankful and lucky to be travelling through that territory. It is a mixture of so many different landscapes. What I loved the most is that the trees are small, which allows for you to see so many breathtaking views. We also stopped at Carcross, where there is a small desert that was created by the last ice age. The Indigenous people of this land have been here for eleven thousand years or more. When we crossed the provincial line into the territory, I looked up some of the Indigenous communities in the Yukon and found out that almost all of the communities are self-governing,[16] which means that each of these communities is responsible for their own resource management, and economic and social programs. They are no longer suffocated and oppressed under the Indian Act. These communities have the power and ability to care for their members and their land in the way they see fit. Out of the fourteen Nations in the Yukon, eleven of them are now self-governing. I encourage you to learn more about this.

In Whitehorse we visited the Transportation Museum. Knowing, before I even stepped into the museum, that the stories told there would be from the perspective of the settler's worldview, I was struck by what brought the settlers there and how they even survived this place. Early photos show settlers arriving in the winter with massive amounts of provisions that they dragged through the mountains on sleds or by foot, in

An environmental microaggression happens when place names and buildings are named after white colonial settlers to the territory.

---

hopes to find some gold. Some would get to the river just as it froze over for the winter and then have to wait until the spring for it to thaw to travel. What a huge amount of patience and foolishness they had. Clearly from the pictures that were displayed, the settlers were not equipped for or knowledgeable about the land and how to survive on it. Many of them did not survive.

Before 1889, the Indigenous people of the Yukon followed the food and the seasons. Life on this land was hard but they learned how to live off the land and sustain their way of life for more than eleven thousand years. When the gold rush hit, settlers hoping to get rich quick populated this land. Indigenous people supported them as guides and teachers of how to survive on the land. This also was the time when the fur trade dwindled. Once the gold rush dried up, the majority of the settlers dispersed, and the Indigenous people went back to their way of life.

It wasn't until World War II that the situation drastically changed for the Indigenous people of the Yukon. The Americans were terrified that the Japanese would attack them from the north, so they believed that they needed a road to get to the north to protect "their" land. The Alaska Highway was commissioned, and the army was to build it.

A very complex history unfolded, during which the government harmed the land, the people of the land, and other minority people who were dragged up to this location. The book *We Fought the Road* by historians Christine and Dennis McClure[17] describes the racism faced by three Black army regiments building the Alaska Highway. The Black soldiers that were brought in to build the road were not allowed to eat and sleep with the white soldiers. Plus, part of the work of the Black soldiers was to build cabins for white soldiers, while they were only permitted to sleep in tents in minus-forty-degree weather. Black soldiers were not allowed in the hotels or restaurants during this time. They were also never photographed in any of the promotional materials shared about the great highway construction project.

There was never a plan to connect with the Indigenous communities to get permission to build a highway through their territories. More than ten thousand American soldiers just arrived in an onslaught to plough through the land. The goal was to build the road as fast as possible. They sent out survey crews with Indigenous guides, then sent in the bulldozers that tore down anything in their way. The path they carved out of the landscape was fifty to ninety feet across. Then the road-building crew came to build the road. The terrain was so difficult to navigate that once crews finished areas they were working on, they left behind trucks, barrel cans, and many other things they did not want to carry out. Still to this day, eighty years later, you can see them lining the road. You can go to my website, carolynroberts.net, to see a photo that I took of one that we saw.

For the highway to be built, the trees, flora, fauna, and people who lived with and on this land were displaced. It altered migration patterns of animals, which disrupted the food supply. It killed trees and flora of the areas, also disrupting the food supply and medicines. When the military came, the soldiers brought diseases like influenza, whooping cough, dysentery, and tuberculosis, all of which killed off 50 percent of the Indigenous population. The Indigenous people did not build the road. They guided the settlers using their walking trails and dog sled trails as the location where the road would be built. Indigenous women were hired to cook and do laundry for the army men that had man camps all along the way of the new highway. We know from the report of the National Inquiry into Missing and Murdered Indigenous Women and Girls that man camps are one of the most dangerous and violent places for Indigenous women. In these camps, the men used animals as target practice, which drastically impacted food sources for the Indigenous people.

The lives of the Indigenous people were never the same after the highway was built. As our tour guide in the Transportation Museum told us, "Colonization was much easier when you had a road." The accessibility of transport made it so much easier for the government to steal children from their home communities to assimilate them in the residential schools.

As told to us in the museum, to the Canadian/American settler eyes, this looked like the greatest highway ever built. It was built in under two years over this vast wilderness. But through an Indigenous lens, this highway decimated the way of life for the First Peoples of this land. It changed the landscape for the animals, trees, and plants. The building of the road killed off the Indigenous population and allowed for easy access to steal Indigenous children.

When we're talking about histories, we need to be mindful of whose side of the story we are reading or telling. How we talk about the history of a place matters, whose voices are shared in history matters, and whose voices are missing matters. Making the connection to the Barkerville story, we must be mindful that we need the stories of all who have been here to fully understand the history of this place now known as Canada today.

Likewise, what we teach, share, and the stories we tell in the classroom matters just as much as how we teach. Bringing in multiple perspectives will support the Re-Storying of this land. If we only hear settlers' stories, then we will only know about their struggle and accomplishments. Like in the case of the museum, leaving out the story of how the settlers' actions decimated a population and destroyed the land.

I hope that by reading this story, you gain curiosity about where you live and the stories that are being told and not being told about the land today.

Practice: Land and the Whole Story

Take the time to do some research about the whole history of the land you are on. Focusing on the Alaska Highway, my questions are:

- Is it really the greatest road ever built?
- What was the cost of the road being built for the Indigenous people, the animals, the land, the flowers, and the trees?
- How can we make sure as educators that we include the Indigenous voices in all we teach?

Connecting this to your location, you could choose a popular location near you. Find out the story of how it came to be today. Then start digging to discover the cost of having that place there today, from the perspectives of the Indigenous people, the animals, the land, the flowers, and the trees.

I Saw the Sign

Another thing we saw on our trip was signs: signs, signs, everywhere signs. We saw so many along the road talking about the history of this land we drove on. Almost all of them were about the gold rush trail and the colonial narrative of this land. But what I personally did not see was even one provincial sign that talked about the Indigenous peoples of this land. I was hugely disappointed with this lack of acknowledgement of the Indigenous history along the way.

If, when teaching in classrooms, we don't teach about the rich history of the locations we live on, then students never learn about and understand the fight for Indigenous land rights. When it is purposefully not taught, the peoples whose voices are silenced have an even more difficult challenge in fighting for what is rightfully theirs. The lack of signs and education about this land purposefully silences voices and knowledge.

Some places do seem to be trying but I feel they could be missing the mark. For example, in Prince George with its "Welcome to Prince George" sign. As you can see from the image below, the colonial name of "Prince George" (this name is an environmental microaggression; please refer back to the "Hell's Gate" section for a definition) is written in massive letters, while in small letters at the bottom of the sign are the words "Ts'uhoont'i Whuzhadel," meaning "welcome" in the Dakelh language of the land. A newspaper story written about the sign talks about how proud the city was that the Indigenous language was included.[18] Using a critical lens when looking at the sign, we can see that being included isn't really what the sign is saying. It is clearly stating that the colonial name is way more important because of how big the letters are and putting the colonial name first, meaning that is the focus of the sign. Then in small letters at the bottom of the sign is the voice of the Indigenous people. This isn't really being included; this sign demonstrates that the colonial name and history are still the dominant narrative and priority of this place.

CITY OF PRINCE GEORGE

The "welcome" sign that emphasizes the colonial perspective.

On the last leg of our trip, we came down Highway 99, and this is where the signs were different. It has a lot to do with the Squamish Nation and how hard it has worked on making sure the language of the land is seen and heard on their territories. These signs honour the language and the people of this place. As you can see in the image below, the Squamish language is on top and the colonial name is in smaller print below. You can see the signs and learn how to say the place names on the Ta na wa Ns7éyx̱nitm ta Snew̓íyelh (Language & Cultural Affairs) Facebook page. This is what inclusion looks like for Indigenous peoples and voices; their voice is first, and in larger print. The colonial voice is in smaller print and after the Indigenous voice.

THOMAS MCILWRAITH

Shisháyu7áy / Britannia Creek road sign that foregrounds the Squamish language and place name.

Highway of Tears

For me, the most unsettling part of this whole trip was driving on Highway 16, known in Indigenous communities as the Highway of Tears. When we turned onto this highway from Highway 37, my heart dropped, and I could feel a massive heaviness. I could not help but think of all the Indigenous women and girls that have died along this highway. It was my understanding from the Highway of Tears report that was created in 2006[19] that along this stretch of highway there were to be signs, billboards, and educational information about this crisis. We did not see this along this route. I saw one red dress hanging, and some signs of missing Indigenous women only in locations of Indigenous Nations. But I did not see anything along this route that told the story of what has happened and continues to happen along this deadly stretch of highway. If we are going to tell the story of this place, we need all of the story. Not just the parts of the story that make people happy and want to be proud Canadians.

As we can see and learn from our own education system, Canada has a long history of lying to us by omission. Why is the story of this highway not noted along this route, when a report written nearly two decades ago called for it? You know the staggering fact from chapter 1 that Indigenous women are four times more likely than non-Indigenous women to be victims of violence. Each one of those women is someone's daughter, someone's mother, someone's sister, or someone's aunty. Why are we not spreading the word and making this known so that we can have the tools and resources to stop it? Billboards and memorials, and educational stops along this route, could educate those who travel this route, with the hope that if they see something that doesn't feel right for them, or see a young Indigenous female hitchhiking, that they would know to call for help, or check in with her. Or other options that the educational material could provide people.

We cannot keep omitting the horrendous history that this country was built upon. We need to educate about the truth just as much as we educate about the gold rush. Collectively we all need to do better; demand better of those who write the signs along the highways; demand more information, more education, so that we can have a better understanding of this place that we all live in today. Things won't get better if we continue to ignore the sad and upsetting parts of our collective history.

Practice: Language of the Land

Here are some ideas that I think could help support students learn about the language of the land:

- Bring your class to a park or historical site and review the signs. Ask students what they think the signs are telling them and what more information they need to know about the location.
- Whose voice is being shared in this story of the signs found in the location you took your class to and whose voice is missing from this sign?
- Have the students do some research on the area to learn more about the history of this land prior to contact.
- For an assignment, you could have the students create new signs for around the school or parks in the community that tell more of the story of where they go to school. Connect with the people of the territory and see where you can learn the names of the locations in the ancestral language so that this can be put on the sign as well, if the location had a name.

Questions for Reflection

- How can you support hearing the differing worldviews of all those who surround you, as an educator or school leader?
- When teaching about the gold rush and other such histories, whose voice do you centre in the teaching? What voices could you include to get a broader understanding of what happen and the impact it had on the land and Indigenous people?
- From the stories in this chapter, what connections are you making to the places that you love to visit or live?
- What do you know about the Indigenous people who lived on the land where you live?
- How can you find out more of the Indigenous history of this place?
- How will you engage your class in learning about the history of the land prior to contact?

Resources

Coté, Charlotte. *A Drum in One Hand, a Sockeye in the Other: Stories of Indigenous Food Sovereignty from the Northwest Coast*. Seattle, WA: University of Washington Press, 2022.

Grenz, Jennifer. *Medicine Wheel for the Planet: A Journey toward Personal and Ecological Healing*. Toronto: Knopf Canada, 2024.

Kimmerer, Robin Wall, and Monique Gray Smith. *Braiding Sweetgrass for Young Adults: Indigenous Wisdom, Scientific Knowledge, and the Teachings of Plants*. Minneapolis: Zest Books, 2022.

Manuel, Arthur, and Grand Chief Ronald Derrickson. *The Reconciliation Manifesto: Recovering the Land, Rebuilding the Economy*. Toronto: James Lorimer & Company, 2017.

"What Is #LandBack? Inside New Native American TV Shows." YouTube video featuring Taietsarón:sere "Tai" Leclaire and Liza Black. Uploaded by @pbsorigins, June 13, 2022. 09:39:00. https://www.youtube.com/watch?v=Q8ePZ46eTDO.

7

Applying a Critical Lens

Decolonization is rooted in the principle of equal rights and self-determination of peoples. It aims to dismantle the dynamics and effects of settler colonialism—which dispossessed Indigenous peoples of their lands, resources, traditions, and culture—to build fairer social, political, and economic structures.

PUBLIC SERVICE ALLIANCE OF CANADA,
"Decolonizing Labour"[1]

PLAYLIST

"Canada, It's Time for Land Back," video explainer with Pam Palmater, from The Breach: Journalism for Transformation

"Miracle," music video, song by Supaman, featuring Maimouna Youssef

"Indigenous Connections to the Land," video by Alannah Young Leon and Francine Burning

"One World (We Are One)," music video by IllumiNative

Scan this QR code for links to these videos.

ONE OF THE assignments that I give my preservice educator students is to create a decolonial lesson plan. At first when I ask students to do this work, there are a lot of big eyes and tension in the room because they do not yet fully understand what I am asking them to do. The key to putting together a decolonial lesson plan is bringing a critical lens and looking for other perspectives within the lesson.

When students come into my class, they have been "marinated"[2] in the western colonial education system for at least seventeen years. Asking them to look with a critical lens is a big ask, because they are not taught how to be critical in the system. Creating lesson plans with a critical lens takes time and practice. With scaffolding like I will provide in this chapter, I have seen success with so many of my students doing this work in teacher education.

In this chapter, I'll walk you through some things I talk about with my class to develop a critical lens for decolonial lesson plans. Let's start with Sumas Lake.

What about the Lake?

This first topic opens up conversations about how and what we share in lesson plans.

In the fall of 2021, just after a massive flood that closed roads, flooded farms, and completely cut off the lower mainland of BC from the rest of BC, a commercial ran on TV. It was from a local grocery store. The opening of the commercial talked about catastrophic rains that had devastated communities and washed away generations of agricultural work in BC. The commercial then concluded with talking about how the grocery store was supporting the farms through this difficult time.

In my classrooms, I ask the students to think about what the commercial is saying and I write out the script so we can all see it. The story is that the rains caused the floods. But it is leaving out some very important information about this story.

A key missing point is that the flooded farmlands were once a lake. Settlers drained the lake and created farmlands. Some of the reasons for this were because the area was known for flooding and had massive amounts of mosquitoes that would feed on the livestock. In some cases the massive amounts of mosquito bites would kill the livestock with how much blood was taken from the animals. In the mid-1920s, settlers created a pump system, dykes, and diverted streams and rivers in the area so that the lake would be gone. Since 1924 the pumps run every day, 24/7, so the land could be free of water and be farmed. It was said that they still found sturgeon, which is a large fish that has survived from the times of dinosaurs, in farmers' crops years after they drained the lake, because sturgeon can live out of water and in mud for long periods of time. There are also colonies of birds that have not been seen since the draining of the lake. The draining of the lake destroyed the way of life for the local Indigenous people of the Sumas Nation, and for the wildlife; it also destroyed the ecosystem that supported the area.

Another fact missing from the commercial was that the atmospheric rivers of rain that contributed to the flood were caused by the climate emergency we are in today on this planet. The commercial just said "catastrophic rains," not "why" they were happening. The climate emergency is a key piece of knowledge that everyone needs to recognize, to hopefully change this for the next generation.

I use this commercial to demonstrate what happens when educators leave out critical points in lesson plans. Sometimes, the "mainstream" story or widely held beliefs that we base our lessons on leave out so much that they are almost not the truth. If we had only ever heard this commercial's version of those floods in BC, we would never know the true story of this land. Being critical educators, we need to add to the story, the history of the people of this land, the land, and the lake itself—and also speak to the climate emergency we are in. This is how we become critical educators and teach the truth about this land.

From talking with people who live around the area known as Sumas Prairie today, so many had no idea that the Sumas Prairie was actually Sumas Lake. I would think that this would also be some critical information to know before buying a house or operating a farm on this land!

Some books to learn more about the lake and the importance of it for the Indigenous people of this territory are *Before We Lost the Lake: A Natural and Human History of Sumas Valley* by Chad Reimer and *Semá:th X̱ó:tsa, Sts'ólemeqwelh Sx̱ó:tsa Great-Gramma's Lake* by Thetáx̱ Chris Silver et al.[3]

Practice: Decolonize a Lesson with a Critical Lens

A critical lens will support you to decolonize your thinking, lessons, and practice. Building that lens you will need to understand how to approach the work. The Public Service Alliance of Canada states within their work: "To effectively decolonize, it is essential to deconstruct the perceived superiority of Euro-Western knowledge and ways of life. In Canada, decolonization calls for an understanding and recognition of Indigenous history, including the acknowledgement that this country has been built on the legacy of colonization, displacement, and erasure of Indigenous peoples."[4] With this in mind, we can take steps to change the narrative in our classrooms.

When I give my students the following exercise, I start with a lesson that centres the western colonial narrative, or only speaks to one perspective, or doesn't centre the students in the class or include the voices of historically silenced people. I have them review the lesson and look for what is missing—missing voices, missing historical information, missing other perspectives, etc. For me this is a decolonial way of approaching the work. If we can see where the pitfalls are and know where to fill in the spots, then we have tools that support us in this work. If I were to only give students a good lesson plan to follow, I wouldn't be helping them learn the tools they will need to be critical. I would be giving them tools to copy. I want the students to be able to understand what decolonizing work is and to be able to do it on their own, through their own lens, so that they can rely on themselves as a critical educator.

Choose a lesson. To start this work with my students, together we look on the internet for a lesson plan (because you can find lesson plans on anything there), and then we read through the lesson, look at it closely, and ask some critical questions:

- Whose voice is heard in this lesson? Whose voice is at the centre of this lesson?
- Whose voices are missing from this lesson?
- Will students be able to see themselves in this lesson?
- Are there other perspectives that might be missing?
- Are there connections to the land, and the peoples of the land, that can be included?

Identify patterns and whose voice is central. These questions help you see whose voice is central in the lessons you teach. If you see a pattern within your lessons, for example, if there

I want preservice educators to understand what decolonizing work is and to be able to do it on their own, through their own lens, so that they can rely on themselves as a critical educator.

---

seems to be always the same voice centred in the lessons, then this is where you can start to shift the narrative being taught. The single narrative is what we are trying to move away from—any one dominant narrative is problematic in a classroom. As you now know, students need windows and mirrors in their work. Windows to see other worldviews, perspectives, and knowledges, and mirrors to see themselves.

The following list shows excerpts from a lesson plan about dams and what the lesson was asking teachers to teach, along with critical questions teachers should ask themselves to identify missing voices. Teacher candidates would be working on materials like this as they are building their critical eye about lesson plans. You can use it as an example of how to do this process yourself.

What the lesson says: Understand the difference between dams and weirs, through classroom discussion.

Critical questions/changing of view: What are the effects of dams on the natural environment? Who has been displaced in the process of building dams? Why are dams built?

What the lesson says: Appreciate that dams are a great place to enjoy recreational activities while, at the same time, having an awareness of the potential dangers.

Critical questions/changing of view: Whose voice is centred in this lesson? Who are dams created for? Who benefits from dams? And who has been harmed or displaced? How is the dam honouring the land as a relation, or kin?

What the lesson says: Look at and understand the purpose of dams, weirs, and water channels and how the water supply is used.

Critical questions/changing of view: What is the purpose of the colonial dam system? How was the waterway used before the dam was built? How does the natural environment support life before the dam? Where do dams occur in the natural environment? Could this lesson be harmful to students? Is the dam the livelihood of families in the class or the whole community? Do all students in the class have access to clean drinking water?

What the lesson says: Have a class discussion about where water comes from when we turn a tap on at home.

Critical questions/changing of view: How does water support not only humans but the more-than-humans as well? Do you know that each of your students have access to tap water at home? If not, how will you address this conversation?

What the lesson says: Discuss how the water got into the dam. What would happen to the level of water in the dam after long periods of rain or long periods of drought?

Critical questions/changing of view: How does changing the natural environment affect climate change and the land, the water, and the more-than-humans? Why would someone want to displace the humans and more-than-humans to benefit only some of the people of the place? Where do the animals go? What happens to the fish? What happens to the trees, flowers, and fauna?

What the lesson says: Ask students to think about the various uses for the water, and who might use it (towns, farmers, industry).

Critical questions/changing of view: Why does this lesson list only towns, farmers, and industry? Why are we focusing on the colonial lens? Let's look at the land before the dam and how that supported all life, then after the dam was built and how it now supports the commodification/monetization of the water and energy from the water.

IF WE ONLY EVER talk about the dam and water for the benefit of humans, we are missing out on so many other perspectives.

Some other questions to think about when creating a decolonized lesson: When considering the curriculum, what social norms, values, and worldviews support the selection of knowledge that you are teaching about? When creating a lesson, how can you ensure that it is learner-centred work? How are you including in the lesson the identities of the students in your classroom? Could the lesson be harmful to students in the class?

It is also important to think about how you communicate and reflect from your own position within society (like we spoke about in chapter 2). How does that show up in the curriculum and how you teach it? When I think about this, I consider the amount of privilege I have as an educator. I have a stable job. I own a house and a vehicle. My family is well taken care of and we have food security in our home. I am also cisgender and heterosexual. This allows a great deal of privilege in the society we live in. Yes, I do not have access to all privileges, but I still come with a lens of privilege and not all my students come in with the same amount of privilege as me. This means I must be extra mindful for where I have blank spots in my learning and understanding. I need to continue to push myself to learn more about my blank spots so that I can make sure I am aware and can include other perspectives in my lesson planning and teaching.

THE QUESTIONS and examples in this chapter show you how to start using a critical lens to support decolonizing your lesson plans. Know that this work is challenging and won't always be easy to spot, but as you do it more, you will be able to see your own blank spots and the missing pieces in your lessons more easily. From here, we can look at how to decolonize assessment.

Questions for Reflection

- How can you start to include Indigenous voices in your lesson plans?
- What are some ways that you are now thinking about decolonizing your lesson plans?
- What are you still wondering about within these conversations?
- How can you use the steps given in this chapter to help support your learning to decolonize?

Resources

Battiste, Marie. *Decolonizing Education: Nourishing the Learning Spirit*. Saskatoon, SK: Purich Publishing, 2013.

Cote-Meek, Sheila. *Colonized Classrooms: Racism, Trauma and Resistance in Post-Secondary Education*. Halifax, NS: Fernwood Publishing, 2014.

Donald, Dwayne Trevor. "Forts, Curriculum, and Indigenous Métissage: Imagining Decolonization of Aboriginal-Canadian Relations in Educational Contexts." *First Nations Perspectives* 2, no. 1 (January 2009): 1–24.

Ferguson, Katya Adamov, and Sara Florence Davidson. *Teacher Guide for the Sk̲'ad'a Stories: Intergenerational Learning and Storytelling in the Classroom*. Winnipeg, MB: Portage & Main Press, 2022.

M'Lot, Christine, and Katya Adamov Ferguson, eds. *Resurgence: Engaging With Indigenous Narratives and Cultural Expressions in and beyond the Classroom*. Winnipeg, MB: Portage & Main Press, 2022.

8

Shared Learning and Assessment

We understand the world around us as being in a constant state of flux and change, ephemeral and shape-shifting. The concept of truth, that there is one absolute way of knowing that never changes, doesn't assist in understanding our environment, and doesn't allow for adaptation to the constant change inherent in that environment.

HAROLD R. JOHNSON[1]

PLAYLIST

"Rock Your World," music video, song by Chubby Cree

"Show Us the Way," music video, presented by N'we Jinan Artists

"Home to Me/Grassy Narrows First Nation," music video, presented by N'we Jinan Artists

"Bimaachiihiiwassuu/Cree Nation of Wemindji," music video, presented by N'we Jinan Artists

Scan this QR code for links to these videos.

I HAVE BEEN working alongside educators all over British Columbia and the Northwest Territories in decolonizing teacher practice, and one of the most common questions I get is, How can we decolonize assessment? This is a complicated question because I believe that assessment practice is a larger conversation in and of itself. So, know that what follows is only a short review into what it looks like for me when I think about assessment. In this chapter, I explain some of the connections I am making with my teaching practice and including some of my conversations with educators over the last few years.

Before we get into the conversation about assessment, I would like to reiterate that colonized education is based on the structure of power. This hierarchy of power is based on the western colonial education model. It was made by white settlers, for white settlers. The history of education here in Canada is rooted in assimilation and colonization. Recall that Egerton Ryerson, the "father of the public education system" in Canada, also created the blueprint for the Indian Residential School System, using residential schools as a tool of assimilation for all Indigenous children. Knowing that the two systems were built by the same person puts into perspective our own education, and what was purposefully left out of our learning. It also shows us the importance of our role as educators, if we want to be change-makers and active participants of change.

That the current public education system is problematic for non-white students has been well documented. The key for understanding the inequities within our system is relationships—relationships are at the core of decolonized teacher practice. Decolonizing the system will require building relationships with students, families, and the school community.

Connecting to students and understanding who they are and how they learn will support you in understanding how to assess their learning, as a process of learning together and co-creating the assessment process with students. This process-oriented practice will take time and constant reflection. But it supports students in finding their own voice and their own strengths. It allows for students' self-expression, which can include their culture, history, and worldview. It can also include their anger, their frustration, and their joys.

The purpose of decolonizing the assessment process is to invite students in as collaborators. Being a part of the process allows students to think through how they express themselves best. It can also challenge students to hold themselves accountable in the work they choose to do by giving them a role in determining their own success. Co-creating assessment takes away the colonial hierarchy of power that the current system is built on. The colonial process of the teacher deciding what, how, and when a student learns leaves out the most important parts of learning: who the student is and how they learn. Sharing in the learning process asks students to acknowledge that they have a role to play in their success. We learn and grow more together.

Practice: Considering Assessment

At this point, you may be hoping that I will give you a checklist for decolonizing assessment. I am sorry to let you down, but I won't be doing that. Each student and each assessment will look different because everyone approaches teaching and learning differently. What I can do is offer you some questions and ideas for approaching the work of decolonizing assessment.

What are you teaching? Start by taking some time to think about what you are teaching, and then create ways that you can invite students into being co-creators of the learning process:

- What do you want the students to know and how will you engage them in learning?
- Are your students reflected in the curriculum you are teaching?
- Can students see themselves within the work or relate to the work they are being asked to do?
- How are you asking students to show up in their work?

How can learners be co-creators? Inviting students into the assessment process as co-creators of learning gives them agency over their learning. Taking the time to discuss with students about how they show their understanding best, and building together an assessment tool for the end goal that supports understanding and makes expectations clear for all students, will support success.

How can students show you their learning? This means inviting in multiple ways of sharing learning, in addition to written output, including videos, podcasts, visual art, oral presentations, and so on. Allowing choices gives students agency.

Holding Ourselves Accountable

Decolonizing education is an ongoing practice that we can do every day in our roles. We just have to hold ourselves accountable to reflect and check in with our work on a continual basis. This means we must *Stop, pause, reflect, repeat*... over and over.

Allow for the space to make mistakes and learn from them.

As I think more about assessment, I think about my personal learning journey with weaving, and my practice as a beginner weaver. If someone were assessing my progress of me learning to weave, their assessment could either encourage me to do better or it could make me feel like a failure. When I am learning about weaving, and the weaving process, I am watching a weaver, I am asking questions, and I am a part of the process of creating. Then I try what they have shown me, and this allows me the space to ask more questions, and to try. Making mistakes and unweaving is part of this process. If the teacher graded me on my progress by saying, "Well, it looks like your lines are wrong or your tension is off, so you fail" or "Here's your bad mark," this would have an impact on my ability to try again. I may just say, "Well, this is too hard. I'm not going to try anymore because my teacher says I am doing badly." This does not allow for the space to make mistakes and learn from them.

Most important for me as a weaver is to learn from my mistakes, learn from practising the process, and to receive constant feedback, so that I can improve my work. Knowing that a given piece is just one of many that I will create over time, I learn from it and put that learning into my next one. Knowing that there are many things that I will need to learn along the way in weaving is important. Knowing that I can always ask questions and that mistakes are part of the process also allows me grace as a student. Understanding that I will not do it perfectly the first time, the second time, or maybe even the thirtieth time gives me room as a learner to keep trying and know that all of the work is part of the learning process.

What if we thought this way in the education system? What if we removed the need to always be right, the imperative to do things only one way, and the pressure of being perfect? How could this support the students and their learning? I believe that this would open up spaces for students to be more curious, to try things they might not be good at. It would allow them opportunities for learning more than what we thought they would learn.

Since assessment is still evolving for me as an educator, I only have a couple of recommendations for this chapter. I will continue to research and learn more, and look for resources that I will link to on my webpage.

Questions for Reflection

- What are some creative ways you have worked with assessment?
- What are the lessons you have learned about in your own assessment practice?
- What was the biggest learning you have done from a mistake?

Resources

Freire, Paulo. *Pedagogy of the Oppressed.* Translated by Myra Bergman Ramos. 50th anniversary edition. Bloomsbury Critical Education. New York: Bloomsbury Academic, 2018.

hooks, bell. *Teaching to Transgress: Education as the Practice of Freedom*. London: Routledge, 1994.

CONCLUSION
I Hope

I THOUGHT THAT you might want to hear why I do this work in Re-Storying Education. I am a huge fan of Monique Gray Smith, and her book *I Hope* is always one that I hold dear to me.[1] I do this work because I have *hope*. I believe that the change-makers in these next generations will be able to move mountains and make more change than I could ever dream of. This is because of educators like you, the ones who wholeheartedly step into this work with an open heart and mind. Because of you, the next generations will be able to be the change needed in education. Because of you, I have hope. Thank you for taking this journey with me through the different ways that you can step into this work in Re-Storying Education. I know the challenges that come with trying to shift educational practice and my hands are raised for those of you who are brave enough to be the change-makers in the system today.

I have hope even though I know how hard this work is and the challenges we face to uplift the voices of those who have been historically silenced in educational systems. I do this work for my grandchildren and the seven generations to come. My ancestors walk with me in this work and watch over me as I push against systems, and moments that I need to take a pause and reflect, so that I can have the energy to try again. I know that the next generations will have a better experience than I did and even better than my children are having now. This work is heavy lifting and heart work, which makes it hard work. I know that not everyone is ready to step in and be disrupters, but I encourage you to be brave and strong and try. This can look like small steps every day toward a different practice in your classroom. A very dear friend of mine, Jenn Calado, always tells me, "Take small steps but many." I hope that this book has brought you some new energy to support you in this work.

Finally, at the end of this work, I would like to offer you a playlist while you reflect and respond to the work.

PLAYLIST

"I Hope" from The Chicks. I heard this song for the first time from Monique Gray Smith.
She played it at a talk and it really affected the way I want to move in this work. The lyrics speak of our children watching and seeing what we do; they trust us, that we will be the ones to give them what they need. It also speaks to listening to history, so we won't make the same mistakes. The hope is love and joy.

"Love Wins" from Carrie Underwood.
I played this song on repeat when I worked for my Nation as the principal of our elementary school. I believed that the song's message was meant to connect us back to who we are. The lyrics speak of all of us being related as sisters and brothers, holding each other up, and love always wins.

> **"We Were Here"** from Aysanabee.
> This is such a powerful and beautiful song of remembrance of who we are as Indigenous people. It speaks about how Indigenous peoples have always been here and are still here with the blood of our ancestors running through our veins.
>
> *Scan this QR code for links to these videos.*
>
> 

Little Bit Better

The last piece I will leave you with is from a fierce Michi Saagiig Nishnaabeg author, Leanne Betasamosake Simpson. This is part of her short story of "for asinykwe."[2] In these final lines of the story, she is speaking of a woman who is healing and repairing the world around her one step at a time. There is no better way to end but with the hope, resilience, healing, and the possibility of a better future.

> she never asked for any recognition, because she wasn't doing it to be recognized. she did it because it filled her up.
> she just carefully planted those seeds.
> she just kept picking up those pieces.
> she just kept visiting the old ones.
> she just kept speaking her language and sitting with her mother.
>
> she just kept on lighting that seventh fire every time it went out.
>
> she just kept making things a little bit better, until they were.

Acknowledgements

MY WRITING of this first book would not have been possible without the love and support of so many people who have allowed me the space to learn and grow as a human and an educator. I hope you know that there are so many people who have brought me to this labour of love that I wouldn't have enough space to acknowledge everyone, but know there are so many people I am thankful for.

First, I would like to thank my children and husband, Bill, for their love and support throughout this project. Their faith in me and their patience in me constantly talking and working through ideas are endless. For that, I am eternally grateful for my family. This work has always been about my children and my future grandchildren. They are my reason for being. I also would not have the voice I have today without the ancestors who have come before me. Their blood runs through me as does their wisdom and knowledge. I am so thankful for all of those who always stand with me in all the work I do. I would also like to thank my family and extended family for their love and support.

I would also like to thank Sara Davidson for being such a good human and a support for me throughout so many parts of my teaching journey. I could not do the work I do today without her support and friendship. I also would like to thank Kau'i Keliipio. She is so kind, gentle, and strong, and I love sharing stories with her and learning from her how to be in this world. She has shown me grace, kindness, and love, and I am eternally thankful for having her in my life.

I would also like to thank my super fangirl Deena Kotak—she reminds me all the time that I am strong and brilliant. I feel like we all need a super fangirl in our lives.

I also know that without the support of so many strong Indigenous women, I would not have the voice I have today. I would like to thank Michelle Pidgeon, Jennifer Grenz, Chas Desjarlais, and Shelly Niemi for their never-ending love and support.

I believe we also need people in our lives that allow us to be fully ourselves, allow us to vent, and allow us to laugh until our belly hurts. This, for me, would be my friend Jody Miki. She is my go-to person when I feel like I cannot do any more heavy lifting. Thank you for being there for me.

I also have had the privilege to work with so many amazing educators that have helped shape who I am. Thank you for always pushing me and questioning me to become a better educator. I would also like to thank so many wonderful schools and school districts all over the province and Northwest Territories that I have had the privilege to work with over the years. They have invited me to work with their Indigenous education teams, admin teams, teachers, and CUPE staff. This work has been so fulfilling and inspiring with all the work people are doing to change the education system. I always feel so privileged to join the conversations and give ideas and support in how we can change education.

I would also like to thank my editor Kendra for walking with me in shaping this book to be the best it can be. She gave me unending support, asked many questions, and provided suggestions that have made this book better—I am so thankful for her.

I believe that all people in my life have shaped me and helped me be the person I am today in this world. I feel like I would not have been brave enough to use my voice had it not been for my dad who raised me. He always told me that if I wanted change, I needed to be an active participant of change. With those words embedded into my being, he guides all that I do. I am forever grateful for both my mom and dad. They have both passed, but I know they are still with me and watching over me.

It has been an honour and gift to be an educator who creates ripple effects in the system. I take this responsibility seriously and hold it with great care. Thank you to all of you who have supported me and continue to support me in this work.

Notes

A Note from the Author

1 Dwayne Trevor Donald, "Forts, Curriculum, and Indigenous Métissage: Imagining Decolonization of Aboriginal-Canadian Relations in Educational Contexts," *First Nations Perspectives* 2, no. 1 (January 2009): 1–24.

2 Leanne Betasamosake Simpson, *As We Have Always Done: Indigenous Freedom through Radical Resistance* (Minneapolis: University of Minnesota Press, 2017).

Welcome

1 Verna J. Kirkness and Ray Barnhardt, "First Nations and Higher Education: The Four R's—Respect, Relevance, Reciprocity, Responsibility," *Journal of American Indian Education* 30, no. 3 (May 1991): 1–15, https://www.jstor.org/stable/24397980.

2 Rudine Sims Bishop, "Mirrors, Windows, and Sliding Glass Doors," *Perspectives: Choosing and Using Books from the Classroom* 6, no. 3 (Summer 1990): 9–11, available from https://scenicregional.org/wp-content/uploads/2017/08/Mirrors-Windows-and-Sliding-Glass-Doors.pdf.

3 "Chief Oren Lyons on Doctrine of Discovery," YouTube, uploaded by @7GenFund, October 13, 2010, 14:44:00, accessed February 25, 2024, https://youtu.be/yVZDbqh7WgM?si=YNumFMflwMM7fg6x.

4 Marie Battiste, *Decolonizing Education: Nourishing the Learning Spirit* (Saskatoon, SK: Purich Publishing, 2013).

5 Elder Xwechtaal Dennis Joseph with Tracy Laslop, "Ah Ni Na—Two Eyed Seeing," YouTube, uploaded by @VCHhealthcare, April 22, 2022,

07:13:00, accessed March 18, 2024, https://youtu.be/SmwqXJMe3io; Fawn Wood feat. Randy Wood and R. Carlos Nakai, "Remember Me," track 3 on *Kikāwiynaw*, Canyon Records, August 28, 2015, provided to YouTube by A-Train Entertainment, August 29, 2015, 04:33:00, accessed March 18, 2024, https://www.youtube.com/watch?v=3-UKIhCQ-C4.

Chapter 1: History

1 *Encyclopaedia Britannica*, "Duncan Campbell Scott," accessed March 21, 2024, https://www.britannica.com/biography/Duncan-Campbell-Scott.

2 Truth and Reconciliation Commission of Canada, "The History, Part 1: Origins to 1939," vol. 1 of *Canada's Residential Schools: The Final Report of the Truth and Reconciliation Commission of Canada* (Montreal and Kingston: McGill-Queen's University Press, 2015), 77–78, https://ehprnh2mwo3.exactdn.com/wp-content/uploads/2021/01/Volume_1_History_Part_1_English_Web.pdf.

3 P.H. Bryce, *The Story of a National Crime: Being an Appeal for Justice to the Indians of Canada* (Ottawa: James Hope & Sons, 1922), https://caid.ca/AppJusIndCan1922.pdf.

4 H.B. Hawthorn, *A Survey of the Contemporary Indians of Canada: Economic, Political, Educational Needs and Policies*, 2 vols. (Ottawa: Indian Affairs Branch, Information Canada, 1966), https://caid.ca/HawRep1a1966.pdf.

5 First Nations and Indigenous Studies, "The White Paper 1969," Indigenous Foundations, First Nations and Indigenous Studies, University of British Columbia, 2009, https://indigenousfoundations.arts.ubc.ca/the_white_paper_1969/.

6 National Indian Brotherhood/Assembly of First Nations, *Indian Control of Indian Education: Policy Paper Presented to the Minister of Indian Affairs and Northern Development* (Ottawa: Assembly of First Nations, 1972), https://oneca.com/IndianControlofIndianEducation.pdf.

7 Royal Commission on Aboriginal Peoples (RCAP), *Looking Forward, Looking Back*, vol. 1 of *Report of the Royal Commission on Aboriginal Peoples*, 5 vols. (Ottawa: Royal Commission on Aboriginal Peoples, 1996), 197, https://data2.archives.ca/e/e448/e011188230-01.pdf.

8 Tabitha de Bruin, "Kanesatake Resistance (Oka Crisis)," *Canadian Encyclopedia*, July 11, 2013, https://www.thecanadianencyclopedia.ca/en/article/oka-crisis.

9 *Beans* (EMA Films, 2020).

10 Royal Commission on Aboriginal Peoples (RCAP), *Report of the Royal Commission on Aboriginal Peoples*, 5 vols. (Ottawa: Royal Commission on

Aboriginal Peoples, 1996), available from https://www.bac-lac.gc.ca/eng/discover/aboriginal-heritage/royal-commission-aboriginal-peoples/Pages/final-report.aspx.

11 The Indian Residential School Settlement Agreement (IRSSA) is available at "Settlement Agreement," Residential Schools Settlement Official Court Notice, n.d., https://www.residentialschoolsettlement.ca/settlement.html. For more on the IRSSA, see Crown-Indigenous Relations and Northern Affairs Canada (CIRNAC), "Indian Residential Schools Settlement Agreement," Government of Canada, Reconciliation, June 9, 2021, https://www.rcaanc-cirnac.gc.ca/eng/1100100015576/1571581687074; and Indian Residential School History and Dialogue Centre (IRSHDC), "The Indian Residential School Settlement Agreement," Indian Residential School History and Dialogue Centre [University of British Columbia], Learn, n.d., https://irshdc.ubc.ca/learn/the-indian-residential-school-settlement-agreement/.

12 Indian Residential School History and Dialogue Centre (IRSHDC), "Grollier Hall Closes," Indian Residential School History and Dialogue Centre [University of British Columbia], Collections, accessed March 15, 2024, https://collections.irshdc.ubc.ca/index.php/Detail/occurrences/206.

13 Truth and Reconciliation Commission of Canada, "Truth and Reconciliation Commission of Canada: Calls to Action" (Winnipeg, Manitoba, 2015), https://www2.gov.bc.ca/assets/gov/british-columbians-our-governments/indigenous-people/aboriginal-peoples-documents/calls_to_action_english2.pdf.

14 Jorge Barrera et al., "Beyond 94: Truth and Reconciliation in Canada," Beyond94: Truth and Reconciliation in Canada, March 19, 2018, https://www.cbc.ca/newsinteractives/beyond-94/.

15 National Inquiry into Missing and Murdered Indigenous Women and Girls, *Reclaiming Power and Place: The Final Report of the National Inquiry into Missing and Murdered Indigenous Women and Girls*, 2 vols., 2019, available from https://www.mmiwg-ffada.ca/final-report/.

16 Assembly of First Nations, "Missing & Murdered Indigenous Women & Girls," Rights & Justice, https://afn.ca/rights-justice/murdered-missing-indigenous-women-girls/.

17 Verna J. Kirkness and Ray Barnhardt, "First Nations and Higher Education: The Four R's—Respect, Relevance, Reciprocity, Responsibility," *Journal of American Indian Education* 30, no. 3 (May 1991): 1–15, https://www.jstor.org/stable/24397980.

18 First Nations and Indigenous Studies, "Royal Proclamation, 1763," Indigenous Foundations, First Nations and Indigenous Studies, University of British Columbia, 2009, https://indigenousfoundations.arts.ubc.ca/royal_proclamation_1763/.

19 Stan Persky, ed., *Delgamuukw: The Supreme Court of Canada Decision on Aboriginal Title* (Vancouver: Greystone, 1999).

20 The Indian Act is available from https://laws-lois.justice.gc.ca/eng/acts/i-5/.

21 Bob Joseph, *21 Things You May Not Know about the Indian Act: Helping Canadians Make Reconciliation with Indigenous Peoples a Reality* (Port Coquitlam, BC: Indigenous Relations Press, 2018).

22 Robert Irwin, "Reserves in Canada," *Canadian Encyclopedia*, May 31, 2011, https://www.thecanadianencyclopedia.ca/en/article/aboriginal-reserves.

23 Robert Matas, "Squamish Band Settles Claim for $92.5-Million," *Globe and Mail*, July 25, 2000, https://www.theglobeandmail.com/news/national/squamish-band-settles-claim-for-925-million/article1041312/.

24 Royal Commission on Aboriginal Peoples (RCAP), *Report of the Royal Commission on Aboriginal Peoples*, 5 vols. (Ottawa: Royal Commission on Aboriginal Peoples, 1996), available from https://www.bac-lac.gc.ca/eng/discover/aboriginal-heritage/royal-commission-aboriginal-peoples/Pages/final-report.aspx.

25 Indigenous Services, "Indian Status," administrative page, Government of Canada, November 25, 2008, https://www.sac-isc.gc.ca/eng/1100100032374/1572457769548.

26 First Nations and Indigenous Studies, "Indian Status," Indigenous Foundations, First Nations and Indigenous Studies, University of British Columbia, 2009, https://indigenousfoundations.arts.ubc.ca/indian_status/.

27 Murray Sinclair, *The Dean's Distinguished Lecture with Senator Murray Sinclair*, filmed November 19, 2019, at Robert H. Lee Alumni Centre, University of British Columbia, Faculty of Education, at 1:05:00, https://educ.ubc.ca/deans-distinguished-lecture-senator-murray-sinclair/.

28 *Simon v. The Queen*, [1985] 2 SCR 387, https://scc-csc.lexum.com/scc-csc/scc-csc/en/item/93/index.do. See also Fisheries and Oceans Canada, Government of Canada, "The Marshall Decisions," March 4, 2021, https://www.dfo-mpo.gc.ca/fisheries-peches/aboriginal-autochtones/moderate-livelihood-subsistance-convenable/marshall-overview-apercu-eng.html.

29 Sarah Ritchie, "Federal Enforcement in N.S. Fisheries Dispute 'Political': Mi'kmaw Lawyer," Global News, September 20, 2021, https://globalnews.ca/news/8204388/liberals-fishery-dispute-mikmaw-lawyer/;

Michael MacDonald, "Conflict over New Indigenous Lobster Fishery Continues to Smoulder amid Some Progress," Global News, December 19, 2022, https://globalnews.ca/news/9358479/indigenous-lobster-fishery-conflict-progress/.

30 Kory Wilson and Colleen Hodgson (MNBC), "The Indian Act," in *Pulling Together: Foundations Guide* (Victoria: BCcampus, 2018), 49–52, https://opentextbc.ca/indigenizationfoundations/chapter/the-indian-act/.

31 Ka'nhehsí:io Deer, "Why It's Difficult to Put a Number On How Many Children Died at Residential Schools," CBC News, September 29, 2021, https://www.cbc.ca/news/indigenous/residential-school-children-deaths-numbers-1.6182456.

32 Doug Cuthand, "Peasant Farm Policy," *Canadian Encyclopedia*, May 27, 2021, https://www.thecanadianencyclopedia.ca/en/article/peasant-farm-policy.

33 Sinclair, *Dean's Distinguished Lecture*.

Chapter 2: Journey through Education

1 Michael Marker, "Theories and Disciplines as Sites of Struggle: The Reproduction of Colonial Dominance through the Controlling of Knowledge in the Academy," *Canadian Journal of Native Education* 28, nos. 1–2 (December 10, 2021): 102–10, https://doi.org/10.14288/CJNE.V28I1-2.196361.

2 Margaret Eby, "Why 'The Outsiders' Still Matters," *Rolling Stone*, April 26, 2017, https://www.rollingstone.com/feature/why-the-outsiders-still-matters-50-years-later-194014/.

3 Province of British Columbia, "Composition 10," BC's Curriculum, accessed March 18, 2024, https://curriculum.gov.bc.ca/curriculum/english-language-arts/10/composition.

4 Province of British Columbia, "Composition 10."

5 Dorinda J. Carter Andrews et al., "Beyond Damage-Centered Teacher Education: Humanizing Pedagogy for Teacher Educators and Preservice Teachers," *Teachers College Record* 121, no. 6 (June 2019): 1–28, https://doi.org/10.1177/016146811912100605.

6 Susan D. Dion, "Disrupting Molded Images: Identities, Responsibilities and Relationships—Teachers and Indigenous Subject Material," *Teaching Education* 18, no. 4 (December 2007): 329–42, https://doi.org/10.1080/10476210701687625.

7 Dion, "Disrupting Molded Images."

8 Derald Wing Sue, *Race Talk and the Conspiracy of Silence: Understanding and Facilitating Difficult Dialogues on Race* (Hoboken, New Jersey: Wiley, 2015).

9 Felicia Rose Chavez, *The Anti-Racist Writing Workshop: How to Decolonize the Creative Classroom* (Chicago: Haymarket Books, 2021).

10 Verna J. Kirkness and Ray Barnhardt, "First Nations and Higher Education: The Four R's—Respect, Relevance, Reciprocity, Responsibility," *Journal of American Indian Education* 30, no. 3 (May 1991): 1–15, https://www.jstor.org/stable/24397980.

Chapter 3: Colonialism in the Classroom

1 Daniel Heath Justice, *Why Indigenous Literatures Matter* (Waterloo, ON: Wilfrid Laurier University Press, 2018), 48.

2 Paulo Freire, *Pedagogy of the Oppressed*, trans. Myra Bergman Ramos, 50th anniversary edition, Bloomsbury Critical Education (New York, London, Oxford, New Delhi, and Sydney: Bloomsbury Academic, 2018).

3 Dwayne Trevor Donald, "Forts, Curriculum, and Indigenous Métissage: Imagining Decolonization of Aboriginal-Canadian Relations in Educational Contexts," *First Nations Perspectives* 2, no. 1 (January 2009): 1–24.

4 Leanne Betasamosake Simpson, *As We Have Always Done: Indigenous Freedom through Radical Resistance* (University of Minnesota Press, 2017).

5 Nel Noddings, "The Caring Relation in Teaching," *Oxford Review of Education* 38, no. 6 (December 2012): 771–81, https://doi.org/10.1080/03054985.2012.745047.

6 Shawn Wilson, *Research Is Ceremony: Indigenous Research Methods* (Halifax, NS: Fernwood Publishing, 2008).

7 Cindy Blackstock, "The Breath of Life versus the Embodiment of Life: Indigenous Knowledge and Western Research," *World Indigenous Nations Higher Education Consortium* 4, no. 1 (2007): 67–79.

8 Niigaanwewidam James Sinclair, "K'zaugin: Storying Ourselves into Life," in *Centering Anishinaabeg Studies: Understanding the World through Stories*, ed. Jill Doerfler, Niigaanwewidam James Sinclair, and Heidi Kiiwetinepinesiik Stark (East Lansing, MI: Michigan State University Press, 2013), 81.

9 Timothy J. San Pedro, "Silence as Shields: Agency and Resistances among Native American Students in the Urban Southwest," *Research in the Teaching of English* 50, no. 2 (November 2015): 132–53, https://doi.org/10.58680/rte201527599.

Chapter 4: Hidden Curriculum

1. Leona Okakok, "Serving the Purpose of Education," *Harvard Educational Review* 59, no. 4 (December 1, 1989): 406, https://doi.org/10.17763/haer.59.4.j774101814p68423.
2. Zoe Tennant, "The Dark History of Canada's Food Guide: How Experiments on Indigenous Children Shaped Nutrition Policy," CBC Radio, *Unreserved*, April 18, 2021, https://www.cbc.ca/radio/unreserved/how-food-in-canada-is-tied-to-land-language-community-and-colonization-1.5989764/the-dark-history-of-canada-s-food-guide-how-experiments-on-indigenous-children-shaped-nutrition-policy-1.5989785.
3. Ian Mosby, "Administering Colonial Science: Nutrition Research and Human Biomedical Experimentation in Aboriginal Communities and Residential Schools, 1942–1952," *Histoire Sociale/Social History* 46, no. 91 (2013): 145–72, https://doi.org/10.1353/his.2013.0015.
4. Tennant, "Dark History of Canada's Food Guide."
5. Health Canada, "Eating Well with Canada's Food Guide 2007," Canada, January 14, 2021, https://www.canada.ca/en/health-canada/services/canada-food-guide/about/history-food-guide/eating-well-with-canada-food-guide-2007.html; First Nations and Inuit Health Branch, *Eating Well with Canada's Food Guide: First Nations, Inuit and Métis* (Ottawa: Health Canada, 2007), https://publications.gc.ca/site/eng/9.689549/publication.html.
6. Deani Thomas and Jeanne Dyches, "The Hidden Curriculum of Reading Intervention: A Critical Content Analysis of Fountas & Pinnell's Leveled Literacy Intervention," *Journal of Curriculum Studies* 51, no. 5 (September 3, 2019): 601–18, https://doi.org/10.1080/00220272.2019.1616116.
7. Thomas and Dyches, "Hidden Curriculum."

Chapter 5: Re-Storying Educational Practice

1. Hannah Arendt, *The Human Condition* (Chicago: University of Chicago Press, 1958).
2. Daniel Heath Justice, *Why Indigenous Literatures Matter* (Waterloo, ON: Wilfrid Laurier University Press, 2018), 28.
3. Justice, *Why Indigenous Literatures Matter*, 43.
4. See, for example, Stephanie A. Fryberg et al., "Of Warrior Chiefs and Indian Princesses: The Psychological Consequences of American Indian Mascots," *Basic and Applied Social Psychology* 30, no. 3 (September 26, 2008): 208–18, https://doi.org/10.1080/01973530802375003;

Scott Freng and Cynthia Willis-Esqueda, "A Question of Honor: Chief Wahoo and American Indian Stereotype Activation among a University Based Sample," *Journal of Social Psychology* 151, no. 5 (September 2011): 577–91, https://doi.org/10.1080/00224545.2010.507265; and Melissa Burkley et al., "Symbols of Pride or Prejudice? Examining the Impact of Native American Sports Mascots on Stereotype Application," *Journal of Social Psychology* 157, no. 2 (March 4, 2017): 223–35, https://doi.org/10.1080/00224545.2016.1208142.

5 "My Culture Is NOT a Costume | Teen Vogue," YouTube, uploaded by @TeenVogue, October 27, 2017, 04:45:00, accessed March 19, 2024, https://www.youtube.com/watch?v=d6Y5cARFJw8.

6 Chimamanda Ngozi Adichie, "The Danger of a Single Story," filmed July 2009, TEDGlobal2009, https://www.ted.com/talks/chimamanda_ngozi_adichie_the_danger_of_a_single_story.

7 Jesse Wente, *Unreconciled: Family, Truth, and Indigenous Resistance* (Toronto: Penguin Canada, 2022), 164.

8 Wente, *Unreconciled*, 168.

9 "7 Myths about Cultural Appropriation DEBUNKED! | Decoded | MTV News," YouTube, uploaded by @MTVImpact, November 11, 2015, https://www.youtube.com/watch?v=KXejDhRGOuI.

10 Kaniehtiio Horn, "Bannock," CBC Radio, *Telling Our Twisted Histories*, July 12, 2021, https://www.cbc.ca/listen/cbc-podcasts/906-telling-our-twisted-histories/episode/15854441-bannock.

Chapter 6: Learning about the Land

1 Royal Commission on Aboriginal Peoples (RCAP), *Looking Forward, Looking Back*, vol. 1 of *Report of the Royal Commission on Aboriginal Peoples*, 5 vols. (Ottawa: Royal Commission on Aboriginal Peoples, 1996), 4, https://data2.archives.ca/e/e448/e011188230-01.pdf.

2 Emma McIntosh, "What We Mean When We Say Indigenous Land Is 'Unceded,'" *Canada's National Observer*, January 24, 2020, https://www.nationalobserver.com/2020/01/24/analysis/what-we-mean-when-we-say-indigenous-land-unceded.

3 Native Governance Center, "A Guide to Indigenous Land Acknowledgment," October 22, 2019, https://nativegov.org/news/a-guide-to-indigenous-land-acknowledgment/.

4 "Land Acknowledgements: Uncovering an Oral History of Tkaronto," YouTube, uploaded by @locallovemagazine6780, November 5, 2018, https://www.youtube.com/watch?v=voXySM-knRc.

5 Chelsea Vowel, "Beyond Territorial Acknowledgments," *âpihtawikosisân* (blog), September 23, 2016, https://apihtawikosisan.com/2016/09/beyond-territorial-acknowledgments/.
6 Hayden King, "'I Regret It': Hayden King on Writing Ryerson University's Territorial Acknowledgement," interview by Rosanna Deerchild, CBC Radio, *Unreserved*, January 18, 2019, https://www.cbc.ca/radio/unreserved/redrawing-the-lines-1.4973363/i-regret-it-hayden-king-on-writing-ryerson-university-s-territorial-acknowledgement-1.4973371.
7 Suzanne Camp, "Beaded Timeline," Indigenous Education, accessed March 19, 2024, https://www.comoxvalleyschools.ca/indigenous-education/beaded-timeline/.
8 Simon Fraser, *The Letters and Journals of Simon Fraser, 1806–1808*, ed. W. Kaye Lamb (Toronto: Pioneer Books, 1960), 458.
9 Parks Canada, "Fraser, Simon National Historic Person," Directory of Federal Heritage Designations, accessed March 19, 2024, https://www.pc.gc.ca/apps/DFHD/page_nhs_eng.aspx?id=15174.
10 Parks Canada, "Simon Fraser (1776–1862): Backgrounder," Government of Canada, July 4, 2016, https://www.canada.ca/en/parks-canada/news/2016/07/simon-fraser-1776-1862-.html.
11 Justine Jawanda, "Simon Fraser 'The Explorer' and the Problem of Contact History," *scotsinbritishcolumbia* (blog), January 12, 2019, https://scotsinbritishcolumbia.wordpress.com/2019/01/12/simon-fraser-the-explorer-and-the-problem-of-contact-history/.
12 Parks Canada, "Simon Fraser."
13 For more about Sunrise When the Salmon Come, see "The Story of Sunrise When the Salmon Come (Cheryl Chapman) of Barkerville Historic Town & Park," Gold Rush Trail, February 14, 2022, https://goldrushtrail.ca/stories/the-story-of-sunrise-when-the-salmon-come-cheryl-chapman-of-barkerville-historic-town-park/.
14 "Our Story," Barkerville Historic Town & Park, accessed March 20, 2024, https://www.barkerville.ca/ourstory/.
15 M. Gale Smith, "Grease!" *BC Food History* (blog), October 15, 2014, https://bcfoodhistory.ca/ooligan-grease-by-gale-smith/.
16 For more information, see Yukon First Nations Culture and Tourism Association, "Places to Go," Indigenous Yukon, accessed March 20, 2024, https://indigenousyukon.ca/places-to-go.
17 Christine McClure and Dennis McClure, *We Fought the Road* (Kenmore, WA: Epicenter Press, 2017).

18 Darin Bain, "Prince George Welcomes New Welcoming Signs," *My Prince George Now*, July 20, 2022, sec. News, https://www.myprincegeorgenow.com/163650/news/prince-george-welcomes-new-welcoming-signs/.

19 Lheidli T'enneh First Nation et al., *Highway of Tears Symposium Recommendations Report: A Collective Voice for the Victims Who Have Been Silenced*, June 16, 2006, https://highwayoftears.org/wp-content/uploads/2022/04/Highway-of-Tears-Symposium-Recommendations-Report-January-2013.pdf.

Chapter 7: Applying a Critical Lens

1 Public Service Alliance of Canada, "Decolonizing Labour" (Public Service Alliance of Canada, September 23, 2022), 1, https://psacunion.ca/sites/psac/files/2022_nationalindigenoushistory-flyer_en-v4.pdf.

2 Marie Battiste, "You Can't Be the Doctor If You're the Disease: Eurocentrism and Indigenous Renaissance," CAUT Distinguished Academic Lecture, April 26, 2013, 6, https://www.caut.ca/docs/default-source/default-document-library/you-can't-be-the-doctor-if-you're-the-disease-eurocentrism-and-indigenous-renaissance.pdf.

3 Chad Reimer, *Before We Lost the Lake: A Natural and Human History of Sumas Valley* (Halfmoon Bay, BC: Caitlin Press, 2018); Thetáx̲ Chris Silver et al., *Semá:th X̲ó:tsa, Sts'ólemeqwelh Sx̲ó:tsa: Great-Gramma's Lake* (Abbotsford, BC: The Reach Gallery Museum, 2020), https://thereach.ca/wp-content/uploads/2023/04/TR_SemathXotsa_Book_LR_01.pdf.

4 Public Service Alliance of Canada, "Decolonizing Labour."

Chapter 8: Shared Learning and Assessment

1 Harold R. Johnson, *The Power of Story: On Truth, the Trickster, and New Fictions for a New Era* (Windsor, ON: Biblioasis, 2022), 121.

Conclusion: I Hope

1 Monique Gray Smith, *I Hope* (Victoria, BC: Orca Books, 2022).

2 Copyright © Leanne Betasamosake Simpson, "for asinykwe," in *Islands of Decolonial Love* (Winnipeg, MB: ARP Books [Arbeiter Ring Publishing], 2013). Excerpt used with permission.

MICHELE MATEUS, MATEUS STUDIOS

About the Author

CAROLYN ROBERTS is a St'at'imc and Stó:lō woman belonging to the Thevarge family from N'Quat'qua Nation and the Kelly family from the Tzeachten Nation, and she is a member of the Squamish Nation under the Indian Act.

Carolyn is a gifted educator and facilitator, and a powerful storyteller—with a genuine, kind, and welcoming presence. Carolyn's deep passion is clear, with a gentle yet powerful presence when she comes to the stage. She speaks with a fierce confidence and extensive knowledge of Indigenous education, history, and culture. She doesn't shy away from sharing her story of survival, knowing that healing comes from sharing and supporting others to step into the work of Indigenous education and decolonization.

Carolyn has been an educator and administrator for over twenty years and has had many different roles as an educator and administrator in the K–12 public school system, as a First Nations Band School principal, and as a faculty lecturer and assistant professor in higher education. She is an Indigenous academic and faculty member working in the Faculty of Education at the University of British Columbia. Her work is grounded in educating about the Indigenous people of this place known as Canada today and the decolonization of the education system. She works with preservice teachers to build their understandings in Indigenous history, Indigenous education, and antiracism to create spaces for a brighter future for all Indigenous people and the seven generations yet to come in education.

Do you want to keep learning about how to Re-Story Education and decolonize your practice?

Let's keep learning together!

I am always happy to hear from you with questions. You can also book me for keynotes and workshops: carolynroberts.net

For insights and updates about my work, stay in touch:

X @mcarolynroberts

Instagram: Indigenouseducation2023

Facebook: Carolyn Roberts

For additional resources, articles, lesson plans, videos, and playlists, scan the QR code below to visit my website, carolynroberts.net: